WHAT COLOR IS YOUR PARACHUTE?
FOR TEENS

FOURTH EDITION

WHAT COLOR IS YOUR PARACHUTE?
FOR TEENS

DISCOVER YOURSELF, DESIGN YOUR FUTURE,
AND PLAN FOR YOUR DREAM JOB

CAROL CHRISTEN

TEN SPEED PRESS
California | New York

This book is dedicated to the 3.2 million undocumented children and young adults under the age of 24 in the United States and the 1.5 million undocumented teens and young adults in this country who are eligible for the expanded DACA (Deferred Action for Childhood Arrivals). They live in limbo. Without documentation or a pathway to citizenship, few of these young adults can better themselves and provide their communities with needed skills through higher education. Our country needs them. We must do better.

It is also dedicated to the memory of my beloved husband, Joseph C. Risser III, and Max, my canine companion of nearly eighteen years. Frequently, Max was my laptop table while writing the first three editions of this book. I miss them both more than words can say.

Contents

My Parachute

This diagram organizes information about what you want in a job. When it is filled in, use it to guide your research to find jobs you will enjoy. To make it easier to use, photocopy this page and enlarge it. You can also draw a nine-section graphic (including the center) on a very large piece of paper.

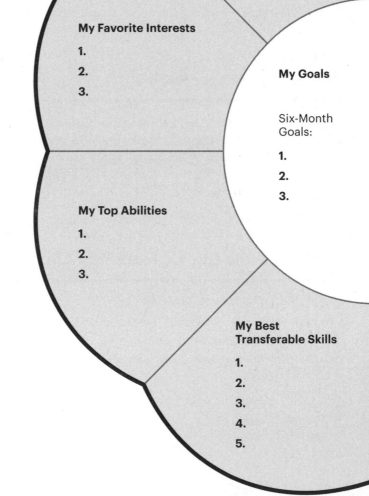

My Best Self-Management Skills
1.
2.
3.

My Favorite Interests
1.
2.
3.

MY PREFERRED SKILLS

My Goals

Six-Month Goals:
1.
2.
3.

My Top Abilities
1.
2.
3.

My Best Transferable Skills
1.
2.
3.
4.
5.

**My Ideal Salary/
Level of Responsibility**

Starting salary:

Ideal salary:

Level:

**My Ideal Work
Environment**

1.

2.

3.

4.

5.

One- to Three-
Year Goals:

1.

2.

3.

Lifetime Goals:

1.

2.

3.

**My Favorite Types of
People**

Holland Code:

☐ ☐ ☐

My Ideal Community

1.

2.

3.

4.

5.

MY PREFERRED ENVIRONMENT

Preface to the Fourth Edition

"Here be dragons" was printed on ancient maps to indicate the unknown parts of the Earth. "Challenges ahead" might be a good warning for the yet-to-be discovered parts of your future. The average employee in the United States works more hours in a year than a thirteenth-century peasant (1,811 versus 1,620!), which means it's very important that you find work you like.

How can you find work you'll enjoy? Make a plan! What you need most to make that plan is time. You can't just order up a career plan like a burger. To make that plan you need time to do research—first on yourself. That kind of research is called self-assessment. Self-assessment leads to self-awareness which leads to good education and career decisions. Research about yourself fills in the Parachute on the previous pages. Once you know the details about what makes a good job for you, you need time to research the world of work to find jobs that match your Parachute. Next, you need time to research your least expensive option for higher education to get the skills and knowledge to start your first career path.

Keep in mind that there is no one path for everyone. It's up to you to create a plan that will build a bridge between where you are today and where you want to be. You don't need to do this work alone. Having an adult that can lovingly keep you on task is a big help. It can take several months to complete your Parachute, research the labor market to find jobs that fit, find higher education you can afford, and create a detailed plan to get you where you want to go. What's the payoff for taking the time to create such a plan? Being a twenty-something living a life you love. Young adults with plans achieve their goals.

This book was written to help you create a plan for your future, and achieve it. The discovery exercises in each chapter will help you learn what you want from life and work and—just as important—how to get it.

Introduction

Putting together a career plan is like solving a puzzle. There are lots of different pieces of information about you and potential jobs that have to be found and sorted through. What bits are high priority for your happiness? What is nice but more like frosting on a cupcake? What's absolutely a no-go? All of these pieces of the puzzle will help you put together a detailed plan for getting the life you want.

Through your school, you may have access to assessments such as The Self-Directed Search, Strong Campbell, or Myers-Briggs. Take them. Assessments can yield clues to your career puzzle. The more clues, the faster the puzzle of your future comes together.

But there's one aspect of *What Color Is Your Parachute? for Teens* that makes it different from standardized assessments: *Parachute* focuses on you and your experiences. Standardized assessments point you toward jobs before you know what makes a job good for you. Through discovery exercises in this book, your previous work and life experiences are examined to find valuable clues to what you need for job satisfaction. Creating your Parachute from the discovery exercises allows you to riffle through your experiences for your likes, dislikes, strengths, abilities, interests, and goals. As you learn about potential careers, your Parachute will encourage you to explore certain jobs and avoid others. The journey to your future is an adventure that holds fascinating discoveries about yourself and how you can build a life you love financed by work you enjoy. Ready? Let's get started.

What Career Planning Is—and Isn't

People who haven't experienced career planning sometimes fear that it will narrow down their options by forcing a decision they'll be stuck with. Good career planning—the kind you're going to learn in this book—will not narrow your options. The Parachute decision-making process is designed to create more, not fewer, choices.

REALITY CHECK

You can do an amazing amount of career work, including reading this book, in just twenty minutes a day.

❝ *Don't worry about failures . . . worry about the chances you miss when you don't even try.* **❞**

—Jack Canfield, coauthor of *Chicken Soup for the Soul*

Discover Jobs You'll Love and How to Get Them

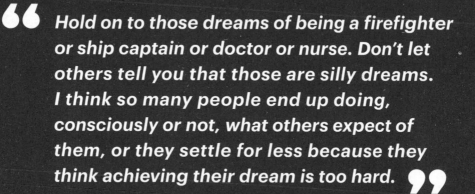

" *Hold on to those dreams of being a firefighter or ship captain or doctor or nurse. Don't let others tell you that those are silly dreams. I think so many people end up doing, consciously or not, what others expect of them, or they settle for less because they think achieving their dream is too hard.* **"**

—Rob Sanders, pediatric physician

The goal of this book is to help you successfully meet the challenges of transitioning from school to work. And not just any work, but a job you enjoy. Surprisingly, the process of finding your first career path can be fun. You'll become a detective looking for clues in your life and in those of others. You'll uncover what matters most to you, what you love to do, the attributes of people with whom you work well, and where you'd like to live. The Parachute form assembles your clues into a blueprint to lead you to work you'll love.

Part one begins your detective work. You'll uncover clues that will answer these three questions:

1. What do you like to do and what are you good at?

2. Who (that is, what kind of people) do you like to do those things with?

3. Where do you want to live and work?

Once you know your what, who, and where, you'll be ready to learn how to find jobs that fit. How is more challenging, so it's covered briefly in part one and in detail in part three. But before that, in part two we'll look at some things you can do right now to get yourself on your way to career success.

REALITY CHECK

Does it seem like everyone but you knows exactly what job they want? It's not true: just 2 percent of adults are working the job their eighteen-year-old selves thought would be their career.

66 *I was lucky—I found what I wanted to do early in life.* **99**

—Steve Jobs, cofounder and CEO of Apple

As you explore what you have to offer, with whom you want to work, where you want to be, and how you can get hired in your favorite field, you'll want somewhere to list your most important discoveries. My Parachute on pages viii–ix brings key career-choice information together in one place. The Parachute is divided into categories that will help you organize what you uncover. When you put all your what, who, and where clues together, you'll have a clear word-picture to guide you in finding work. Your Parachute diagram is designed to steer you toward a job you'll love.

Keep your career work in both electronic versions (computer, external hard drive, or cloud) and hard copy. With this backup, you won't lose your hard work should your computer crash. You'll want to return to your Discovery Exercises often to finish your Parachute, plan for higher education, or campaign to get hired doing work you enjoy. Your answers will change as you accumulate more life and work experience. People with dynamic careers revisit and revise their Parachutes every couple of years.

REALITY CHECK

You may be thinking, "Is all this self-assessment to fill out my Parachute really necessary?" True story: while in college, a woman now working as a college adviser took a common career assessment but did no other self-assessment or career exploration. That assessment said the top job match for her was journalist, so she quickly changed her major to journalism. While in school she had an internship at a small-town weekly, then after graduation she was lucky enough to get a job as a writer for a large daily newspaper. She hated it immediately. The noise level from conversations, constant movement of people delivering copy or messages, and pressure to produce quickly was too chaotic. She tried being a freelance journalist but didn't like working alone and the constant need to travel. After working in a different field for a couple years, she returned to school. She became an academic and career adviser at a community college, where she advocates for students to thoroughly get to know themselves and the work they want to do before declaring their majors.

CHAPTER 1

What You Love to Do: Your Favorite and Best Skills

Why does this first chapter focus on what you love to do? Because what you love to do reveals both interests and skills. Favorite interests and skills, especially those you most enjoy using, are major clues to finding work you'll love. Let's look at your interests first.

Discover Your Favorite Interests

Interests are important because they lead to fields, and fields lead to jobs. Take a moment and think about how you spend your time. Of all the activities you do, which are the most fun? What captures your attention and your imagination? You might not be able to make that part of your job, but what if you could? What is your favorite subject in school? What fascinates you? Everyone will have different answers—his or her unique combination of interests. Danika, for example, loves movies. Jeff spends hours on his computer trying to figure out new ways of doing things. Jessica loves plants and gardening, and Darnel lives and breathes sports of all kinds. So how might these different interests lead Danika, Jeff, Jessica, and Darnel to work they'll love?

Let's take a look at Danika's interests first. If Danika chooses movies or filmmaking as a career, she could be an actress, a screenwriter, a director, or maybe a movie critic (then she'd get to see lots of movies). But Danika has many more possibilities to choose from. She could be a researcher for historical movies, a travel expert that scouts locations, set designer, model builder, a carpenter that builds sets, a painter for backdrops and the like, costume designer, makeup artist, hairstylist, camera operator, lighting technician, sound mixer or editor, composer for soundtracks, a stuntperson, caterer, personal assistant to the director or cast members, an on-site medic, secretary, publicist, accountant, product placement specialist, or any number of other things. The credits at the end of a movie list even more personnel and their roles, although you've got to read fast.

Danika also loves animals and is good at training them. She could combine her interests and become an animal trainer (or "wrangler" as they're sometimes called) for the film industry. That's a job most people wouldn't think of when considering careers in film.

What kind of career might Jeff's interest in computers lead to? He could be a programmer, computer repair person, or video game developer. Or because he loves art as well as computers, maybe he'll work with Danika in the film industry as a computer FX designer, web designer, or illustrator of educational materials. These are just a few of Jeff's job options, depending on his other interests and skills.

Because of her interest in plants and gardening, Jessica could become a florist, botanist, or developer of plant hybrids, she might run her own landscape design, lawn maintenance, or plant nursery business. If Jessica likes to travel, she could be a plant photographer, or search for exotic plants for new medical treatments.

Darnel's love of sports might lead him to be a professional athlete or a coach. Because he loves working with kids and has a little brother with cerebral palsy, he might help children with physical disabilities get the exercise they need by teaching adaptive physical education.

As you see, your interests can lead you in many different directions for work. It's true that interests change with time, age, and exposure to new people, places, and experiences. But it's also true that your interests now may be with you all your life, so naming your current interests is a great starting place for finding work you'll love. Let's take a closer look at your interests now.

REALITY CHECK

Don't worry about picking your big career-for-life now. Focus on finding work you will enjoy that can finance your twenties, and help you save money for more education or training toward that future big career.

How to Find What You Love to Do: Discover Your Favorite Interests

Think about your answers to the questions below and write each answer on a slip of paper or sticky note.

- When you have free time and no one is telling you what to do, what do you like to do?

- What's your favorite subject in school? Second and third favorites?

- When you're in the magazine section of your school library or a bookstore, what type of magazine (computer, fashion, sports, news, and so forth) will you pick up and read first?

- Fill in the blank: When I'm _____, I lose track of time and don't want anyone or anything to disturb me.

- If someone asked you what your favorite interests are, what would you say?

- What are your favorite hobbies, sports, or recreational activities?

- What internet sites are your favorites? What sites do you have bookmarked? What is the subject matter of those sites? What do you pin most frequently on Pinterest?

- What kinds of problems do you like to solve?

- What kinds of questions do your friends or classmates bring to you for help?

- What fascinates you? What could you read about, talk about, or do for hours?

After you've answered all the questions, put your answers in a list. Pick your ten favorites. Write each favorite on a sticky note, slip of paper, or 3 by 5 card. Arrange and rearrange your answers until you've got them in order of preference: your favorite interest first, second favorite next, and so on. Make a prioritized list of your top ten. Write your top three interests in the My Favorite Interests section of My Parachute (page viii). As your interests change, be sure to update your Parachute. (You can also experiment with using an online prioritizing grid to select your favorites. See www.beverlyryle.com/prioritizing-grid.) You've got the first section of your Parachute done. Woohoo! Good work! You're off to a great start.

Discover Your Abilities

> **❝** *The youth of today need to be prepared from an early age for what lies ahead. It starts with the system guiding a young person to focus on areas where he has natural abilities, not because he is lazy and doesn't want to get challenged but because this is an area he is naturally wired for and we don't want him/her struggling later on in life.* **❞**
>
> —Yusuf Olanrewaju, human resources professional, Nigeria, West Africa

Your abilities add important pieces to the puzzle of your future work. Abilities are different from interests or favorite subjects in that they are broader, more subtle, and considerably more important. While interests and favorite subjects change over time, abilities are more permanent. Abilities are the hard wiring of your mind. They form much of your operating system. Interests are more like the programs or apps installed to run on a computer. Abilities determine how your brain works, what information your brain notices and takes in, and how your brain processes that information (which includes data, numbers, pictures, images, and ideas). While you can work to improve any ability, usually your strongest are natural talents that have been with you since birth. Different kinds of work require different skills, and making career choices that take advantage of your strongest abilities will help you become successful.

While working for General Electric in the 1920s, a man named Johnson O'Connor developed one of the first aptitude tests used in the United States, which he later expanded for use by the public. Currently used aptitude tests owe much to this early work, as it measured concept organization, inductive reasoning, structural visualization, numerical reasoning, and foresight. The Johnson O'Connor test is still used but it's expensive. You can take a quick, free online version on Oprah.com in the article Test Your Career Strengths (http://www.oprah.com/omagazine/aptitude-tests-career-assessment/all).

You can also take one of the following ability tests:

- The Armed Services Vocational Aptitude Battery (better known as ASVAB) is the most widely used multiple aptitude test in the world. It tests for arithmetic reasoning, word knowledge, paragraph comprehension, mathematics knowledge, science, electronics, auto repair, and the ability to assemble objects.

- A newer ability test developed by YouScience has quickly become popular in schools here in the United States (www.youscience.com). The code PARACHUTE gives you a 50 percent discount on all ability tests offered.

Standard ability tests take several hours to complete and give you huge amounts of information. Not all that information will fit into your Parachute. If you've taken the ASVAB, YouScience, or other ability test, write your top two or three abilities in the *My Top Abilities* section of your parachute diagram.

REALITY CHECK

Ability assessments are different than interest assessments. Unlike ability tests, questions asked in interest assessments have no right or wrong answer. The ASVAB is a high-quality ability test made available through many high schools for free. Make sure you've thought out your feelings about serving in the military in advance of taking the test. If you score high in abilities needed by any branch of the military, recruiters can be intense and insistent in their efforts to sign you up. You can be flattered, but you needn't be persuaded. Make sure you can say, "Thank you, but I'm not interested," if that's how you feel.

Identify Your Abilities to Find Your Competitive Advantages

Rich Feller, PhD
Professor at Colorado State University
https://richfeller.com

Being accepted within groups and having friends is an important part of being a teen. One way to gain confidence is learning that your unique abilities provide competitive advantages that always show up. While interests explain where you spend much of your time and energy, they change with exposure to new experiences and people. Your skills and self-management are especially important as your aptitudes connect you to careers and jobs that best suit you.

Each career or job requires a different ability mix. Neurosurgeons have different abilities than sports marketing specialists, welders, or data scientists. Thinking on your feet, responding quickly, and enjoying brainstorming sessions may be easy for you. Finding it easy to visualize in 3D, seeing patterns in numbers quickly, and putting things in logical order comes naturally for others. Confirming natural abilities shines light on your gifts, and provides a head start to become your best in your areas of strength. Connecting competitive advantages to your developing interests helps to clarify where success can most easily be found.

Are your abilities different than those of your friends? Consider that different careers/jobs require different abilities. Abilities represent your unique competitive advantages and how your talents best perform within recommended careers/jobs, and assessing them will help you identify your most rewarding and pleasurable ways to perform.

On page 12, review the abilities listed in Column A.

List your name in Column B, and the names of two friends or relatives that you know well in columns C and D.

Estimate which person best performs the Sample Ability in Column A (3 is best, 2 is next best, 1 is third best).

Identify how your abilities are different from others to help you appreciate your natural and unique talents.

(A) SAMPLE ABILITY	(B) YOUR NAME	(C) FRIEND OR RELATIVE #1	(D) FRIEND OR RELATIVE #2
HAND-EYE COORDINATION: easily learn complex movements (e.g. dance, sports) after simply watching others or from visual instructions			
VISUAL COMPARISON SPEED: fill out forms quickly or notice a typo in a sign, menu, or paper			
NUMERICAL REASONING: fascinated by trends in numbers and generally enjoy number games or puzzles			
SPATIAL VISUALIZATION: can visualize how objects would most effectively be organized in a given space			
SEQUENTIAL REASONING: quickly organize a lot of information simultaneously in their heads while listening and talking			
IDEA GENERATION: always have ideas, regardless of how much they've thought about a topic or how much they care about it			
INDUCTIVE REASONING: get to conclusions without having all the information or following a logical step-by-step method of problem-solving			

Using your estimates above, list the three abilities with the highest scores in the My Top Abilities section of your Parachute. If you have ties, pick the three you feel are your best strengths.

Estimates of performance can introduce you to abilities and their value within the Parachute process. Use the code PARACHUTE at www.youscience.com to measure your actual performance using thirteen different ability subtests carefully designed to assess a broad range of abilities employers seek.

Skills You Enjoy Using

In this section, the definition of "skill" is an ability or the expertise to do something well, and your top skills are your best clues to finding a job you love. How? It's simple: when you know what your skills are, especially your best skills, you can look for jobs that use them. It just makes sense that the jobs you're most likely to enjoy will use your favorite skills. There are three different types of skills used in career planning: transferable, knowledge (or interests), and self-management (also called personality traits). The most basic building blocks of any task are transferable skills. Along with your interests and abilities, transferable skills are the foundation for finding what you love to do. Transferable skills are called "functional" skills because these are functions you actively perform with your body or mind. Once hired, you're more likely to keep your job if it involves interests and skills you do well. Why? It's hard to succeed if you don't like what you do. If your job makes you unhappy, you'll want to spend less time at work, not more.

"But I don't have any skills," you say.

Nonsense! You have more skills than you realize. Often our best skills are so close to us that we're not even aware of them. They come so easily and naturally that we think they are nothing special, that everybody has them, or that anybody can use them the way we do. Our skills grow as we grow. As we gain more life experience, overcome challenges, pursue further education, or work at a particular job for an extended period of time, we gain more skills. But by the time you're a teenager, you've already developed several hundred skills. Let's find your favorites.

Transferable Skills

A transferable skill can range from a basic life skill—like being able to turn on a water faucet once we're tall enough to reach it and strong enough to turn the handle—to a more advanced skill, such as the ability to drive a car. While "skills" is the term we'll be using, they are sometimes also called "talents" or "gifts."

REALITY CHECK

It takes a long time to become good at something, so you might as well spend that time becoming good at something that really interests you. Many successful ventures were started by young entrepreneurs following their interests. Check out this article, "Companies Founded by Amazing Young Entrepreneurs" in *Business News Daily*, about fifteen young entrepreneurs who developed their interests into businesses (https://www.business-newsdaily.com/5051-young-entrepreneurs.html). Some of them aren't even in high school yet!

Let's say skateboarding is one of the interests you named earlier. When you skate-board, you work with some "thing" (a skateboard), and skateboarding is what you do with it. What are your transferable skills? You have hand-eye-foot coordination, physical agility, and exceptional balance, as well as the ability to make split-second decisions and take risks. These skills aren't limited to skateboarding; they're also valuable in work as a surfing instructor, aerial performance artist, arborist, search-and-rescue, and many other jobs. That's what makes these skills transferable.

Transferable skills can be divided into three different types: physical, mental, and interpersonal (we use the acronym TIP—Things, Information/Ideas, or People—to refer to all three skill types). Physical skills use the hands, body, or both, and generally involve working with materials, equipment, objects (like a skateboard), even plants and animals. Mental skills primarily use the mind and generally involve working with data, information, numbers, or ideas. Interpersonal skills primarily involve working with people as you serve or help them with their needs or problems. So if one of your skills is skateboarding, your transferable skills include physical skills (hand-eye-foot coordination, agility, balance, and maneuvering) and mental skills (split-second decision making). Skateboarding can also involve using interpersonal skills, espe-cially if you're on a team, or enjoy teaching others how to skateboard.

Why Are My Transferable Skills Important?

Your transferable skills are particularly important as you look for jobs that match your Parachute because they are the building blocks of tasks, and can be used in any field or career you choose, regardless of where you first picked them up or how long you've had them. For example, your ability to swim is a skill that can be used in work as a lifeguard, a swim coach, a counselor at a summer camp, or a US Navy SEAL.

Most jobs rely on certain core activities or tasks that you must complete over and over, and to do them requires certain skills. To perform these activities or tasks well requires the skills you use most often. These groups of skills are sometimes called "skill sets," and it's important to identify yours. Once you know your best transferable skills—the ones you do well and enjoy using—compare them with the skills needed for a particular job. If a job doesn't use three-quarters of your best skills, you probably won't be happy with it. The more your best and favorite skills factor into a job, the more likely you will love it.

PARACHUTE TIP

You may want to photocopy the Skill TIP boxes on pages 19 to 21 before you begin marking the skills you used in your stories. This leaves you with a fresh copy if you want to do this exercise in the future or share it with a friend.

How To Find What You Love to Do: Identify Your Skills

Think back to the last month. Were there any challenges? Did you overcome them? Did you complete any tasks or projects successfully? What were they? Did you enjoy them all, or just certain parts?

You begin to identify your skills by looking at your life. Think about projects you have completed, recent problems that you solved, your hobbies, and the activities you do for fun. These can be experiences from your school, volunteer work, paid work, or free time. Select a challenge, project, or activity you've enjoyed that had an outcome—such as writing a paper, helping to organize an event, or learning a new sport or hobby.

Rich Feller, professor of career development and author of the book *Knowledge Nomads and the Nervously Employed,* says that 70 percent of our skills come from challenges, 20 percent from watching others, and 10 percent from classes and reading. Your story can also come from any of these three categories. If you're stumped about what might make a good skills story, think about challenges you're particularly proud about having overcome. Once you've thought of a story, write a short paragraph that describes how you completed your project or worked out a solution to a problem. (Need a little inspiration on what kind of story to write? See the Student Example on page 16.)

Now give your project, problem, or activity a title. Then answer these questions below.

- Goal or Problem: What was your goal; that is, what were you trying to accomplish, or what was the problem you were trying to solve? Any time you have a goal that challenged you, you'll uncover lots of skills.

- Obstacles: What obstacles made achieving your goal or solving the problem difficult? How did you overcome these obstacles?

- Tasks or Roles: What tasks helped you achieve your goal? Did you fill a particular role—perhaps as a teacher, volunteer, researcher, customer service, or something else?

- Time Frame: How long did it take you to achieve your goal or solve the problem? Using an overlong time frame can often hide skills. We tend to shrink lengthy accomplishments into condensed versions that skip over important skills. If solving a particular problem took several years, choose an especially challenging part of that problem.

- Outcome: What happened? Did you achieve your goal or meet the challenge? Did things go as you expected, or did something unexpected happen? If the outcome is still pending, perhaps choose another story.

Pulling Up My History Grade

David, age 18, high school senior

In order to graduate from high school, I had to pass my history class. I had a poor grade in history because I hadn't spent time studying earlier in the year and couldn't understand the current material. I was told that I wouldn't graduate if I didn't bring my history grade up considerably. I wanted to better myself and graduate high school, so I started going for extra help whenever the teacher offered it. When I stayed after school, I listened to what my teacher said and followed her advice. The material began to sink in. I read the material that was assigned each day and began turning in my homework. I started to do better in the class. However, I had an overdue project that I needed to complete to pull my grade up. The assignment was to write an essay for history on a topic that I wanted to write about. I chose to write about President John F. Kennedy's assassination because I was interested in the topic. I found information on JFK's assassination and then wrote the essay. I was proud of myself because I earned a B on the assignment. I also graduated on time with my class.

Goal or problem: Graduating from high school

Obstacle: Passing mandatory history class and writing an essay

Time frame: Less than 90 days

Outcome: Graduated!

Now that you have read a skills story, are you ready to do a little detective work to write your own? Let's turn to your life and begin to identify your skills—your favorite skills, especially.

Discover Your Transferable Skills

Your skills story can come from any part of your life. David's story deals with school; yours could be from a job, volunteer work, a sport, or hobby. First, give Skills Story #1 a title. Then start identifying the goal or problem followed by the obstacles, time frame, and outcome of your story. Then, write a paragraph or two about how you achieved your goal—this could include noting which tasks helped you achieve your goal, or a particular role you had to fill. If you're writing on paper, leave a couple inches blank on one side for listing the skills you used to make your outcome happen.

Now, reread your story and find and list the skills involved. Take a close look at words that end in -*ing*. These words are called gerunds, and they indicate that you are do*ing* something. Now, reread your list of skills in this story before setting it aside. Because trying to match your list of skills to the Skill TIP boxes on pages 19 to 21 is beyond frustrating, it's much easier to go the opposite way: look at each skill described in the TIP box, and mark box #1 for the transferable skills you used in your first story. All of the skills in these boxes are transferable, and can be used in many different settings or jobs.

For example, if you noted "making" as a skill in your story because you made a presentation to your chess club, put a check mark in box #1 underneath "making presentations in person" on the Skills with People page (page 21, third column over, third box down).

Let's go back to David's story: what skills did David use to achieve his goal of graduating?

- **SKILLS WITH THINGS (PHYSICAL):** David used finger dexterity and hand-eye coordination to type on a computer keyboard, copy information from books or websites, and write his report.

- **SKILLS WITH INFORMATION (MENTAL):** To improve his grade and write his report, David used a variety of skills, including of compiling, researching, copying, organizing, analyzing (how he could improve his grade), prioritizing, planning (a process to achieve his goal), synthesizing (bits of information into a whole report), memorizing, managing his time, making files on a computer, and retrieving that information as needed.

- **SKILLS WITH PEOPLE (INTERPERSONAL):** David's interpersonal skills included receiving instructions, listening carefully, asking questions, communicating well in writing, using words, following through, completing tasks, decision making, initiating, and taking risks.

Now that you've gone through the process and understand how it works, write four more stories so you have a total of five. If you wrote about a school project the first time, try writing about something else: teaching your little sister how to ride a bike, learning to ice-skate, dealing with a friend who gossiped about you behind your back. Your stories can be inspired by work, school, or free time; from this year, middle school, or much earlier in your life. Writing five stories will help you dip into different parts of your life and see what skills you used in a variety of situations. It also lets you see patterns and frequency in how often you use particular skills. Do they show up in one, four, or five stories? The skills that show up most often are likely your best, although they may not all be your favorite. You'll be able to make that distinction later.

You've already written Skills Story #1. Next, write Skills Story #2. Again, leave a blank column for writing the skills you find in your story. Read this column and your story a couple of times. Place check marks in box #2 for each skill you used achieving your goal. Do this for stories #3, #4, and #5. You will find that in each story, you used skills in the "things" category, others in the "information" category, and still others in the "people" category. If you write one story a day and fill in your skills, then in five days you can know what your best transferable skills are—and you'll have two sections of your Parachute done!

When you have all five stories written and their skills marked, look over the Skill TIP pages. Is one page loaded with skills, or are your skills spread evenly over all three pages? Each person's skill patterns are different: don't worry if yours don't look the same as your best friend's.

Summary: Discover Your Skills

1. Write a skills story and reread it a couple times.

2. Identify the skills you used. You can underline the skills, highlight them, or circle them in color.

3. Make a list of the skills you used.

4. For each skill in the Skill TIP boxes, pages 19 to 21, ask yourself, "Did I use this skill in accomplishing my goal?"

5. If this is your first story, check box #1 for each skill you used. Check box #2 for your second story, and so on until you have identified the skills used in each of your five stories.

Skill TIP: Skills with Things

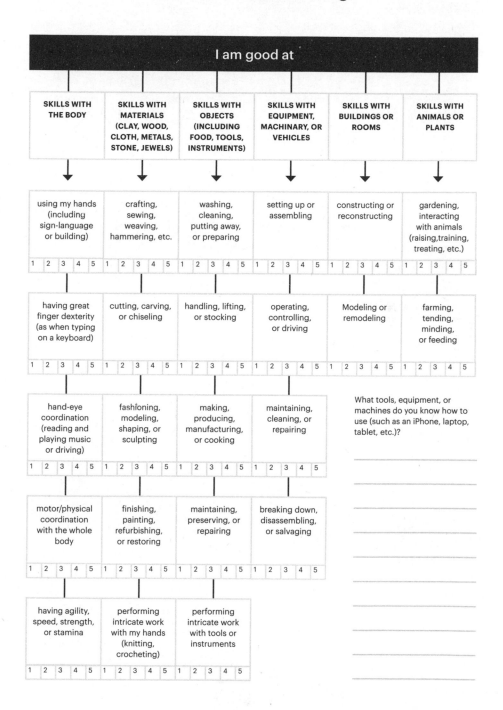

I am good at					
SKILLS WITH THE BODY	**SKILLS WITH MATERIALS (CLAY, WOOD, CLOTH, METALS, STONE, JEWELS)**	**SKILLS WITH OBJECTS (INCLUDING FOOD, TOOLS, INSTRUMENTS)**	**SKILLS WITH EQUIPMENT, MACHINARY, OR VEHICLES**	**SKILLS WITH BUILDINGS OR ROOMS**	**SKILLS WITH ANIMALS OR PLANTS**
using my hands (including sign-language or building)	crafting, sewing, weaving, hammering, etc.	washing, cleaning, putting away, or preparing	setting up or assembling	constructing or reconstructing	gardening, interacting with animals (raising, training, treating, etc.)
1 2 3 4 5	1 2 3 4 5	1 2 3 4 5	1 2 3 4 5	1 2 3 4 5	1 2 3 4 5
having great finger dexterity (as when typing on a keyboard)	cutting, carving, or chiseling	handling, lifting, or stocking	operating, controlling, or driving	Modeling or remodeling	farming, tending, minding, or feeding
1 2 3 4 5	1 2 3 4 5	1 2 3 4 5	1 2 3 4 5	1 2 3 4 5	1 2 3 4 5
hand-eye coordination (reading and playing music or driving)	fashioning, modeling, shaping, or sculpting	making, producing, manufacturing, or cooking	maintaining, cleaning, or repairing		
1 2 3 4 5	1 2 3 4 5	1 2 3 4 5	1 2 3 4 5		
motor/physical coordination with the whole body	finishing, painting, refurbishing, or restoring	maintaining, preserving, or repairing	breaking down, disassembling, or salvaging		
1 2 3 4 5	1 2 3 4 5	1 2 3 4 5	1 2 3 4 5		
having agility, speed, strength, or stamina	performing intricate work with my hands (knitting, crocheting)	performing intricate work with tools or instruments			
1 2 3 4 5	1 2 3 4 5	1 2 3 4 5			

What tools, equipment, or machines do you know how to use (such as an iPhone, laptop, tablet, etc.)?

_____

_____

_____

_____

_____

_____

_____

_____

Skill TIP: Skills with Information

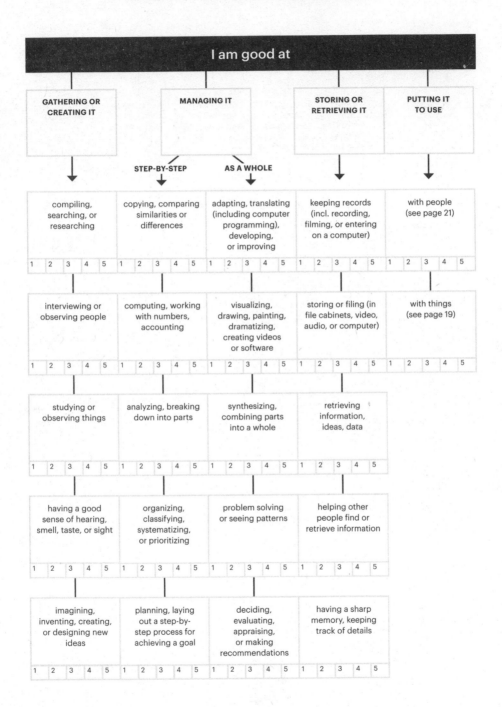

I am good at

GATHERING OR CREATING IT — **MANAGING IT** — **STORING OR RETRIEVING IT** — **PUTTING IT TO USE**

STEP-BY-STEP — AS A WHOLE

GATHERING OR CREATING IT	MANAGING IT (STEP-BY-STEP)	MANAGING IT (AS A WHOLE)	STORING OR RETRIEVING IT	PUTTING IT TO USE
compiling, searching, or researching	copying, comparing similarities or differences	adapting, translating (including computer programming), developing, or improving	keeping records (incl. recording, filming, or entering on a computer)	with people (see page 21)
1 2 3 4 5	1 2 3 4 5	1 2 3 4 5	1 2 3 4 5	1 2 3 4 5
interviewing or observing people	computing, working with numbers, accounting	visualizing, drawing, painting, dramatizing, creating videos or software	storing or filing (in file cabinets, video, audio, or computer)	with things (see page 19)
1 2 3 4 5	1 2 3 4 5	1 2 3 4 5	1 2 3 4 5	1 2 3 4 5
studying or observing things	analyzing, breaking down into parts	synthesizing, combining parts into a whole	retrieving information, ideas, data	
1 2 3 4 5	1 2 3 4 5	1 2 3 4 5	1 2 3 4 5	
having a good sense of hearing, smell, taste, or sight	organizing, classifying, systematizing, or prioritizing	problem solving or seeing patterns	helping other people find or retrieve information	
1 2 3 4 5	1 2 3 4 5	1 2 3 4 5	1 2 3 4 5	
imagining, inventing, creating, or designing new ideas	planning, laying out a step-by-step process for achieving a goal	deciding, evaluating, appraising, or making recommendations	having a sharp memory, keeping track of details	
1 2 3 4 5	1 2 3 4 5	1 2 3 4 5	1 2 3 4 5	

Skill TIP: Skills with People

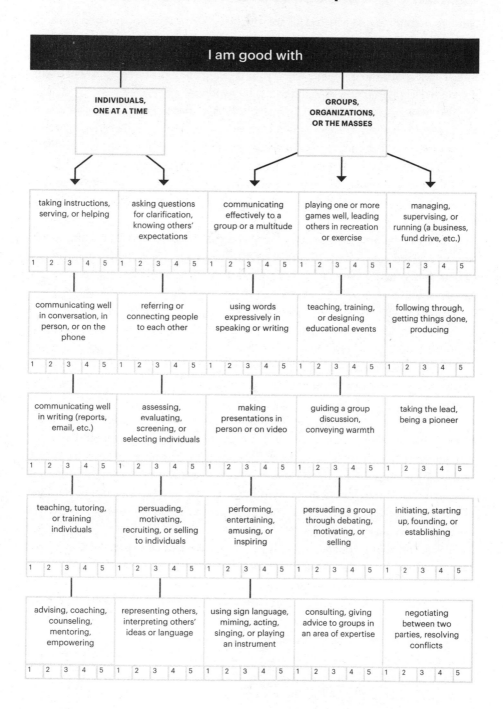

I am good with

INDIVIDUALS, ONE AT A TIME		GROUPS, ORGANIZATIONS, OR THE MASSES		
taking instructions, serving, or helping	asking questions for clarification, knowing others' expectations	communicating effectively to a group or a multitude	playing one or more games well, leading others in recreation or exercise	managing, supervising, or running (a business, fund drive, etc.)
1 2 3 4 5	1 2 3 4 5	1 2 3 4 5	1 2 3 4 5	1 2 3 4 5
communicating well in conversation, in person, or on the phone	referring or connecting people to each other	using words expressively in speaking or writing	teaching, training, or designing educational events	following through, getting things done, producing
1 2 3 4 5	1 2 3 4 5	1 2 3 4 5	1 2 3 4 5	1 2 3 4 5
communicating well in writing (reports, email, etc.)	assessing, evaluating, screening, or selecting individuals	making presentations in person or on video	guiding a group discussion, conveying warmth	taking the lead, being a pioneer
1 2 3 4 5	1 2 3 4 5	1 2 3 4 5	1 2 3 4 5	1 2 3 4 5
teaching, tutoring, or training individuals	persuading, motivating, recruiting, or selling to individuals	performing, entertaining, amusing, or inspiring	persuading a group through debating, motivating, or selling	initiating, starting up, founding, or establishing
1 2 3 4 5	1 2 3 4 5	1 2 3 4 5	1 2 3 4 5	1 2 3 4 5
advising, coaching, counseling, mentoring, empowering	representing others, interpreting others' ideas or language	using sign language, miming, acting, singing, or playing an instrument	consulting, giving advice to groups in an area of expertise	negotiating between two parties, resolving conflicts
1 2 3 4 5	1 2 3 4 5	1 2 3 4 5	1 2 3 4 5	1 2 3 4 5

Identify Your Best Transferable Skills

Now we're ready to find which skills are your "best"—the ones you most enjoy using. Every job will require certain tasks or skills that might not be your favorites. But to find a job you'll enjoy, it's important to know which skills you really like and perform well. Think about the moments when you have big chunks of free time: what skills do you like enough to use over and over, all day long?

You have both "can-do" and "want-to" skills. Can-do skills are ones you don't want to use very often. You carry them with you, and you may even need to use them in your ideal job, but they're not the focus of your work. For example, you probably have the skills to wash all the dishes from a Thanksgiving dinner for thirty people; you might even use your dishwashing skills daily. But how often would you want to use those skills at your job? If the answer is "never," then those skills fall under the category of can-do.

Want-to skills are ones you enjoy using and could do over and over again, several times a day, and not go crazy. It's important to remember that each of us has different can-do and want-to skills, and that's a good thing—the world needs people with a variety of skill sets.

Look at the Skill TIP pages again. Which are can-do skills versus want-to skills? Cross out your can-do skills, the ones you *can* do but don't really *enjoy* using. It might be hard to cross out some of your can-do skills if you are very good at them, and have gotten kudos for using them in the past. Cross them out anyway—you don't want to build a career around can-do skills, as it would bring you little joy in your work.

Now, here's the really fun part: finding your best skills. Go back to the Skill TIP boxes. From the skills that you used in more than one story, select ten to fifteen that you enjoy most. Write each one on a slip of paper or sticky note. As you look at each skill, think about how much you want to use it in your work—often, or just occasionally? Place these skills in order from most to least favorite. This can be hard but give it a try. (If it's helpful to use an online prioritizing grid, go to www.beverlyryle.com/prioritizing-grid.)

Teens and young adults frequently ask if they have to be experts to keep a particular skill on their lists. The answer is no. If you like using a skill and marked it in multiple stories but have a moderate amount of experience with it, keep it on your list of favorites. Remember, it's always possible to develop your skills more fully through education, practice, or concentration.

Now, look at the top five: these are your best and most favorite transferable skills. They are important clues for finding enjoyable work. Write them in the My Best Transferable Skills section of My Parachute on page viii, and feel free to use colored pens or pencils to add a little color to your Parachute!

Summary: Identify Your Best Transferable Skills

1. Review your list of skills. Cross out skills you don't really like using and make a separate list of the rest.

2. Select ten to fifteen skills you enjoy using. Write each on a sticky note.

3. Put the skills in order from most favorite to least favorite, then write them down in order of priority (your favorite first, etc.).

4. Look at your list of skills. The top five are your favorite transferable skills.

5. Write those skills in the My Best Transferable Skills section of My Parachute (page viii).

Self-Management Skills

Neat categories always have exceptions. In your stories, you may have some bits that don't fit into the Skill TIP boxes, but you think they might be skills. They probably are since any one of them could fall under one of the three different skills categories of transferable, knowledge, and self-management.

Transferable skills are the favorites you discovered while writing your five stories and later checked off on the Skill TIP boxes.

Knowledge skills are revealed through your interests, and are also known as work content skills. These skills are what you must *know* in order to do a certain job or activity. To engage in most interests or hobbies, you must have knowledge specific to that activity. For example, a friend of yours knows Korean and is often called upon to translate what grandparents are saying for younger cousins. In this instance, speaking Korean is one of her knowledge skills. In our sample skills story, David applied his knowledge of reading English. If he used a particular program to write his paper on JFK, the ability to use that program is a knowledge or work content skill.

Knowledge skills can be found in interests you already have, and in those you want to study further. You completed these in the section My Favorite Interests on My Parachute (page viii). Your interests involve work content skills that could be useful for your career. If you uncover additional interests through your stories, should you create a new interests list and reprioritize that list? That depends on how much you want a particular interest to be part of your work. Spend some time thinking about your interests, knowledge, and abilities. Divide them into two lists: "Fascinates me" or "Doesn't fascinate me." Prioritize only those that fascinate you.

Self-management skills are also known as personal traits. These traits describe the unique way you manage yourself in relation to other people, and in certain environments—such as the workplace, at home, and in school. Being adventuresome, thorough, energetic, decisive, and compassionate are all examples of self-management skills.

PARACHUTE TIP

Self-management skills employers value most are organization (which includes time management and the ability to prioritize tasks), accountability, adaptability, initiative or self-motivation, and stress management. If you want to become a manager, add problem solving, decision making, and confidence to your self-management repertoire.

In his skills story, David used many self-management skills in the desire to better himself. He is aware of cause and effect: if he improved his history grade, he could get his high school diploma. By reading assignments and handing in homework, he demonstrated follow through. David was aware he was part of the problem—so he analyzed the situation, saw he could do better, and challenged himself to do so. David was self-motivated; he saw the problem and created a workable solution. All of these traits are valued by employers and will help David in his career. When you enjoy your job and the people you work with your self-management skills can help you become efficient, productive, and successful.

The following exercise will help you name some of your self-management skills or personality traits.

Identify Your Best Self-Management Skills

1. Take a few minutes to reread your five stories. When you were overcoming obstacles or achieving your goals, *how* did you do that? Thoroughly, quickly, logically, confidently, independently, or some other way?

2. How did you manage yourself in relation to people, different environments, or time?

3. Which self-management skills or personality traits do you see in your stories? Make a list.

4. What similarities do you notice? Do you see any patterns in how often or in which situations you used certain self-management skills? (Don't worry about being right. Guesses are okay.)

5. Write each trait on a separate sticky note.

6. Organize the sticky notes in order of priority, with your favorite trait first, and so on. Once you've found the right order, make a separate list of these ranked traits. Do some of your favorite self-management traits overlap with the top five self-management skills employers want?

7. Write your top three traits in the My Best Self-Management Skills section of the My Parachute diagram (page viii).

As a young worker, you may not have many specific kinds of knowledge skills, but if you are dependable, punctual, manage your time efficiently, are self-motivated, and work well with others, you can get hired based on your self-management skills. For the really good ones, be sure to talk them up in hiring interviews.

Well, that's done! I hope you had fun too. Now that you know and have recorded your skills across the three category types—favorite interests, best transferable skills, and best self-management skills—on My Parachute, you are more prepared to find and keep a job you'll enjoy. If you filled in the Abilities section, you've got over half your Parachute in working order.

The Discovery Exercises in chapters 1 and 2 guide you through uncovering and naming your skills. Did you learn something about yourself that you didn't know before? Did an exercise confirm something that you sensed?

PARACHUTE TIP

Self-management skills are of great interest to employers. There are lots of blogs, articles, and videos online where you can find lists of self-management skills, learn their importance to your career, and discover how to improve the ones you have. Now you know you've got lots of different skills, all of which you can list by name. Knowing your skills means you can talk about them in hiring interviews and use them to sell yourself to an employer. In the next chapter, you'll discover which types of people are good to have around when doing what you love for a living. Great coworkers are a big part of job satisfaction because being with people you enjoy helps you do your best work.

EXPERT ADVICE

Tips for Teens and Young Adults with ADHD

By Robin Roman Wright, BCC, career and ADHD coach
www.linkedin.com/in/adhdcoachrobin
coachrobin@leadershipandcareers.com

If you have ADHD, you may be wondering if you can use the Parachute method for finding a dream job. I have worked for many years with teens and young adults with ADHD, and I can confidently say yes, you can. However, you will be more likely to complete this book's activities if you strategize with a trusted adult. This can be a parent, relative, teacher, guidance counselor, career center counselor, or career coach.

When thinking about career planning, one important thing to keep in mind is that school is likely the most restrictive environment in which you will ever have to perform. Many work environments allow for more individual approaches to completing assignments, including the ability to negotiate working conditions, project delivery dates, and even flexible schedules.

The US economy is evolving and changing quickly, providing opportunities for people with the ability to think outside of the box—as many with ADHD do. Individuals with ADHD often have a creative spark, keen interests, and a bountiful curiosity that helps them succeed in the workplace.

Extracurricular activities are of particular importance for teens and young adults with ADHD. These are avenues where you can develop competence and really shine. Experts agree that it's best for people with ADHD to work in a field that fascinates them, so notice and nurture what interests you! Many of these areas and activities will be passing interests and may become future hobbies, but one or two may open doors for you to shine in a future line of work.

CHAPTER 2

Who You Love to Work With: Your Favorite Types of People

---

66 *You can have everything you want in life, but probably not at the same time.* **99**

—Muriel Christen

Your coworkers can make a bad job tolerable or turn a good job into a bad experience. Have you had a part-time or summer job where your work was pretty boring, but you still liked going to work? Did you like going to work because of the people? Did coworkers become friends? Maybe you had a boss who helped you learn new skills. Perhaps you met interesting customers, clients, or patients every day. If you haven't had a job yet, you may have had similar experiences in a class: it wasn't super exciting but your friends were there, the teacher made the subject interesting, or projects took you away from the classroom to meet amazing people.

Most every job you'll have as a young adult will surround you with people. Later in your career, you may work from a home office or out of your suitcase from a laptop as you travel the world. People who are difficult or otherwise make you feel uncomfortable can ruin a good job, but an ordinary, not-so-interesting job can be fun if you enjoy your coworkers.

Finding a job that's the right fit involves more than discovering what you love to do; it also means discovering what kinds of people you enjoy. Let's do that now by going to a party!

The Party

You've received an invitation to a party with people your age or a little older, but you don't know any of them well. If you're wondering, "What kind of party is *that*?!" Don't worry—I promise it'll be fun.

Below is an aerial view of the room where the party is happening. Guests with similar interests have gathered in different corners of the room, and each group is filled with fascinating people chatting with each other.

The terms Realistic, Investigative, Artistic, Social, Enterprising, and Conventional tag each corner (designated by the first letters of each word, R-I-A-S-E-C). The aerial diagram below gives brief descriptions of the people who might be attracted to each letter group. Examples of their specific interests appear on page 29. You'll notice how their interests and skills all work together.

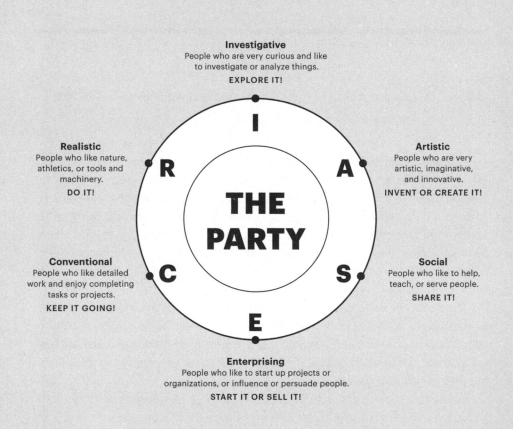

Investigative
People who are very curious and like to investigate or analyze things.
EXPLORE IT!

Realistic
People who like nature, athletics, or tools and machinery.
DO IT!

Artistic
People who are very artistic, imaginative, and innovative.
INVENT OR CREATE IT!

THE PARTY

Conventional
People who like detailed work and enjoy completing tasks or projects.
KEEP IT GOING!

Social
People who like to help, teach, or serve people.
SHARE IT!

Enterprising
People who like to start up projects or organizations, or influence or persuade people.
START IT OR SELL IT!

Examples:

Realistic (R): Tom loves to hike in the mountains and does volunteer trail maintenance. Dee plays on the school soccer team. Paul repairs cars. Louise and Larry build furniture in their father's woodworking shop. Ross grows vegetables for the farmers' market. Yvette raises dogs to be companion animals for people with disabilities.

Investigative (I): People who are very curious and like to investigate or analyze things. *Examples:* Jason always wants to know things like why he no longer sees a certain bird in his area, why the brain works the way it does, why one ball team plays better than another. Jessica investigates the best places to take a date—concerts, movies, amusement parks, hiking trails—and writes about them for her school paper. Erin analyzes everything from the data in her chemistry experiments, to the results of her community-service projects. Ezra is a member of student council who wants to figure out why new students have so much difficulty scheduling the classes they need.

Artistic (A): People who are very artistic, imaginative, and innovative. *Examples:* Ashley draws cartoons. Carlos, Aaron, and Stacy started a band and play at local dances. Guy designs costumes and sets for school theater productions, and is known for creating great stuff with few resources. Daniela develops her own computer animation software. Each of them likes to work in unstructured situations.

Social (S): People who like to help, teach, or serve people. *Examples:* Isabel, a senior, helps first-year students get accustomed to life in high school. Shae tutors middle school students in math and English. Keri volunteers at a food bank. Darin is a trainer for the school football team. Moneesh serves as a peer counselor.

Enterprising (E): People who like to start up projects or organizations, or influence or persuade people. *Examples:* Dana started a service project where high school students visit the elderly in a convalescent home. Ty, who's running for student-body president, started a campaign to convince people to vote for him. Nash persuaded his friends to do volunteer work serving at-risk youth.

Conventional (C): People who like detailed work and enjoy completing tasks or projects. *Examples:* Mika is the treasurer for a service club, and keeps detailed financial records of all its fund-raising activities. Kristin works part-time in an insurance office, where she's responsible for keeping client files updated. Terri oversees planning for the prom, making sure that everything is completed on time.

Okay, now you know a little about who'll be at the party. You've just arrived and walk in the front door. Here are three questions for you:

1. Which corner of the room would you go to first—that is, which group of people would you most enjoy talking to for the longest time? Write the letter for that corner in the first box.

2. After fifteen minutes, everyone in the same corner as you leaves for another party. Among the remaining groups, which corner would you be drawn to the most? Which group of people would you enjoy getting to know next? Write the letter for that corner in the second box.

3. After fifteen more minutes, this second group also leaves for another party. You look around and decide where to go next. Of the groups that remain, which one would you most enjoy hanging out with for the rest of the party? Write the letter for that corner in the third box.

4. The three letters you selected indicate your "Holland Code." Turn back to My Parachute (page ix) and write (left to right) the letters of the groups you chose in the boxes of the section My Favorite Types of People. Then write a short description of your code on a separate sheet of paper. For example, if your Holland Code is *IAS,* you might write: "I'll enjoy my work if I'm surrounded by people who are curious and like to investigate or analyze things (I), who are highly innovative and creative (A), and who want to help or serve people (S)." Include details from My Favorite Interests. Writing a narrative helps you turn letters into a description of the types of people you are most likely to enjoy having as coworkers.

The Party exercise is based on the work of the late John Holland, PhD, who developed the Self-Directed Search. Dr. Holland was a psychologist who did extensive research on work. His studies showed that all jobs fell into one of six occupational themes—Realistic, Investigative, Artistic, Social, Enterprising, and Conventional—and that most individual interests encompass three of those themes. Your Holland Code includes one letter for each theme that represents you, with the first being the most dominant. People who share the same occupational theme also share similar skills, values, and interests—even the same leisure activities and hobbies. Similar jobs attract similar people.

The Party exercise is considered accurate by 90 percent of those who complete it, and more comprehensive than the Self-Directed Search (SDS). If you want to take the SDS, go to www.self-directed-search.com. It takes twenty to thirty minutes, and costs $14.95 for a personalized report listing occupations and fields of study that most closely match your interests.

About Career Assessments

This book is designed to replace career assessments by following clues from your experience. If your school offers free career assessments, take advantage of the opportunity. You never know what piece of information might be the one that solves your career choice puzzle.

Assessments do have limitations, however, especially when it comes to naming your best skills. An assessment suggests jobs based on your answers, but it doesn't know if you've got the skills to do those jobs. This is why writing skills stories is so important, and why a completed My Parachute diagram can be more helpful for making career choices than an assessment. A job title is generic, but your Parachute contains specific details for your career happiness. No assessment can give you a final, once-and-for-all answer about what job would be perfect for you.

Assessments have other limitations. Their databases may be lacking jobs in places where you want to live. Ideally assessments would have thousands of job titles for you to narrow down and choose from, based on your responses, but few assessments actually have more than five hundred jobs in their databases, so the list of suggestions you receive is very limited.

With assessments, the jobs suggested for you are performed by people who answered the questions the same way you did. Those suggestions may not be a great match with your entire Parachute, but they are a good place to begin your investigations. Do some research online or study occupational guides at a library to learn more about each job before nixing it. Instead of getting discouraged if there aren't any suggestions you like, ask yourself: in what field are the jobs that were suggested for you? Does this field interest you, even if the suggested jobs don't? Might there be other jobs in this field that would use most of your skills, or be a better match for your Parachute? Through research and networking (which we'll explore later in the book), you can discover jobs you'll enjoy.

Career Sites for Further Exploration

You can also use your three-letter Holland Code to research job possibilities at career information sites such as O*Net: www.onetonline.org/find/descriptor/browse/Interests/. O*Net has information about nearly 900 jobs and how to train for them. It is free and you may discover interesting jobs you might never have thought of or knew existed. Career research expands your job possibilities.

Below is a list of additional free online career sites. They feature job profiles, employment projects, and training requirements.

- Bureau of Labor Statistics https://www.bls.gov/k12/students.htm

- Career OneStop https://www.careeronestop.org/ExploreCareers/Learn/career-profiles.aspx and https://www.careeronestop.org/GetMyFuture/

- College Grad https://collegegrad.com/careers/all

EUREKA.org is a large, easy to use, well-organized subscription-based career information website. EUREKA provides assessments, information about two thousand different jobs, links to colleges and universities where you can pursue your studies, and advice for parents and job seekers. The site has a variety of job-search resources, including lists of short-term and two-year courses that prepare you for high-wage, in-demand jobs. It's a secure site to store information for your career plans.

Your high school or college may subscribe to EUREKA—check with your career center or guidance counselor to see if EUREKA is available to you. If not, get a few friends together and chip in for a membership. Individual costs for a month are $19.99. A year costs $49.99. Family one-year subscriptions are $99.99. The EUREKA website is worth every penny!

About Bosses

As a teen, you may not have much choice in the attributes and temperaments of your bosses. As you look ahead, discovering that you want to work with a specific demographic for customers, clients, or patients are clues that can point to specific careers. Throughout your work life, knowing what you want from supervisors and coworkers can help you pick one job offer over another. The type of people you work with and for can either stall your career or make it take off like a rocket.

Bosses and Clients

What is your idea of a good boss or manager? Knowing the attributes of your ideal boss will make it easier to recognize one when you meet them. A good boss can be a great mentor. Some teachers are like managers: even though you might not like how hard they make you work, they manage to pull good work out of you and you end up learning a lot from them. When you are just starting out, you want a boss who can help you learn how to be excellent in your field, trade, or craft.

1. Take a piece of paper, fold it in half horizontally, then fold it in half again. Voilà! You now have four columns.

2. In the top left column, write the names of managers, bosses, supervisors, teachers, and short-term project leaders (fellow students included) who you thought were either really good, or really bad. If you don't feel comfortable listing individual names, use job or project titles instead.

3. For the really good leaders, write "liked" or the + sign in the second column and list the attributes you appreciated about each person.

4. Use the third column to write "didn't like" or a – sign, and list the characteristics or behaviors that made it hard for you to do your job.

5. Label the fourth column "A good boss for me" (or something similar) and use it to consolidate your lists. This is about what you're looking for, so turn your negatives into positives—but that doesn't necessarily mean choose the opposite. For example: if you received no supervision, the opposite would be constant supervision, and that's not fun. In this instance, a positive could be, "daily check in for supplies and assignments." So describing what you would have liked is an easy way to translate a negative into a positive.

6. Look at the fourth column. Pick seven to ten attributes that are most important to you and write them each on a sticky note. Arrange them in order of priority. Write "managers" in the My Favorite Types of People section of your Parachute on page ix, then list the top two or three words that describe your ideal boss. Another reason to enlarge the My Parachute diagram!

7. Do this same exercise to create lists of the attributes you most want in your coworkers.

8. Do you know you want to work with specific types of customers, clients, or patients? For example, maybe you want to do physical therapy with children, train horses, or teach seniors how to make nutritious meals.

Put the top items from each list in the people section of your Parachute. If there's no room, draw a line and write along the bottom of the page, add a sticky note, or draw a larger version of your Parachute. A piece of 24 by 36-inch newsprint is ideal for this exercise.

CHAPTER 3

Where You Love to Be: Your Ideal Life and Work Environments

Your heart has its own geography, where it prefers to be. That may be by a mountain stream, or in the Alps. It may be in the hustle of the streets of Shanghai or New York, or the quiet of an Oregon farm. It may be a beach town, or it might be right where you are now—in your own hometown or in your own backyard.

Your soul knows the places it loves. Finding where you most want to live is as important as doing work you love. Imagine having your dream job in a place you abhor—how awful! Living and working where you are happy is an important part of having your best life. It's living your whole dream, not just part of it. This chapter will help you find that place and explore the very important issue of work environments.

> **66** *Happiness, true happiness, is finding the one place in the world where you really want to be.* **99**

—Daphne du Bois

Geography has become more important than ever for career planning. In the United States, one in three young adults doesn't want to move away from the area in which they grew up. The best job market for these young adults to explore is the one in which they live—why look for jobs elsewhere? Dynamic economies with ever-expanding job opportunities exist on both US coasts. But Colorado, Idaho, Iowa, Minnesota, Nebraska, Nevada, New Hampshire, Texas, and Utah also have hopping job markets. In places where the demographics reflect an abundance of young entrepreneurs, recent college graduates, and plenty of openings in existing occupations, new jobs are born.

There are also more educational opportunities on the coasts. Students in rural states where higher education sites are more than an hour away from a community college should look at online learning.

To help you discover your ideal community and work environment, you'll be asked lots of questions. You may have answers for some, but not others, and that's okay—answer what you can. Wait a few days and come back to the ones you didn't answer. Unanswered questions can be useful by making you notice new things and examine possibilities in a way you hadn't before. If asked, "Would you rather work outside or indoors?" and you aren't sure, you may start to notice what types of jobs are done indoors or outdoors, or what jobs combine both indoor and outdoor work. You might think about how you feel after being indoors for several hours, compared to spending the same amount of time outside. Maybe you want to work indoors but on weekends you want to mountain bike, hike, ski, or surf.

Your answers are clues to guide further exploration of where you'd love to live, work, and play. Your answers will change over time as you visit places you've never been before; going away to school or working in new places will expand your ideas about what makes certain locations a good fit for you. Let's start by exploring something you may never have thought about before: your ideal work environment, and what makes it just right for you.

Your Work Environment

If you get a full-time job, roughly one-quarter of your life each week will be spent at work. Some young adults have gotten their ideal job using their best skills, only to find that the workplace is so uncomfortable they must quit. Your work environment needs to be one in which you not only feel comfortable and safe, but also able to thrive. We use the term "environment" here because your ideal "where" includes more than just the location (office, laboratory, farm) where you do your work. Work environment includes the neighborhood in which your work site is located; your workspace (desk, cubicle, lab space, five-thousand-acre ranch, or machine shop); physical conditions (windows or no windows, natural or fluorescent lighting, noisy or quiet); atmosphere (formal, casual, lots or little interaction with people); company size (small, large, local, national, international); and clothing (uniform, suit, jeans, or the latest fashions). Work environments can support or hinder your work style.

When you've visited various workplaces, such as your parent's office, your doctor's office, or your school, what have you liked or not liked? Where do you like to study—in a quiet library, or in your bedroom streaming music, alone, or with a group? In what locations do you feel most comfortable, or uncomfortable? Where would you like to spend more time? The same job (or very similar jobs) can happen in many different environments—some you would love, some you would hate! Let's explore what's right for you.

My Ideal Work Environment

Answer the following questions as best you can, but don't feel that you need to answer them all at once. Set a timer for fifteen minutes. If you're enjoying the exercise when the timer goes off, set it for another ten minutes. Or answer some of the questions now, then come back again in a week and answer more. The second time around, you may notice things that you weren't aware of before. If you think of something not included here, put that on your list, too.

LOCATION: WHERE WOULD YOU MOST LIKE TO WORK . . .
- Indoors or outdoors? In an office building? In a machine shop? On a ranch? At your home?
- In an urban, suburban, or rural area?
- In many locations or one spot (travel or no travel)?

WORK SPACE: WHAT KIND OF SPACE WOULD YOU MOST ENJOY . . .
- A cubicle in a large room with lots of other people in their own cubicles?
- Your own desk in a private office?
- Lots of variety—at a desk, in your car, at clients' locations, on airplanes, in hotels?
- A classroom, laboratory, hospital, garage, workshop?
- Outdoors—golf course? ranch? barn? forest? under the sea?
- A place with all the latest tools, technology and necessary supplies; or a place with limited resources, supplies, and equipment?

PHYSICAL CONDITIONS: DO YOU PREFER . . .
- Fancy and upscale, moderately nice, or does it not matter?
- Windows that open and close or a climate-controlled building?
- A light or dark environment? Natural or artificial light?
- Comfortable temperature or varied temperatures?
- Safe or risky? (What does "safe" mean to you, and what might you need to feel relaxed and able to do your best work?)

ATMOSPHERE: DO YOU PREFER . . .
- Noisy or quiet? Calm or bustling?
- Formal or casual—for example, do you want to call your coworkers "Ms. Smith" and "Mr. Jones," or do you prefer that everyone is on a first-name basis?
- Lots of contact with coworkers or very little?
- Lots of contact with the public (clients, patients, customers) or very little?
- A hierarchical setting (where the boss tells everyone what to do) or a collaborative setting (where the staff works together to determine goals, priorities, and workload)?

SIZE/TYPE OF BUSINESS: DO YOU PREFER . . .

- Large or small? (Think about what "large" and "small" mean to you.)
- Locally-owned, national, or multinational? For profit or nonprofit organization?
- Knowing all your colleagues and customers, or always having a chance to meet someone new?
- Running your own business?

CLOTHING: WHAT WOULD YOU LIKE TO WEAR AT WORK . . .

- A suit?
- Trendy clothes?
- Casual, comfortable clothes?
- A uniform (such as a military, firefighter, police officer, or restaurant server)?
- A lab coat?
- Whatever you want to wear?

In addition to answering the above questions, you can use the list of all the work or volunteer jobs you made in the Discovery Exercise about bosses and clients on page 33. This time, list the working conditions you liked or disliked. Turn the dislikes into positives and create a combined list. Compare your responses to the questions above. You can combine working conditions from the above questions with your like/dislike list.

From the questions above, gather a list of ten items, including at least one from each category: Location, Workspace, Clothing, Atmosphere, and so on. Write each item on a sticky note and rank them by importance. Select your top five factors and write these in the My Ideal Work Environment section of My Parachute (page ix).

Your Ideal Community

You and your friends have different ideas of what makes a great place to live. Ski fanatic? You'll want to be within easy distance of the mountains. Love to surf? A coastal surfing community would suit you. One friend may want to live near a lake, river, or desert. Another may want to live near good friends or family. Do you have excellent foreign language skills (or want to develop them)? You may want to live in another country.

What about transportation? Want to work within a few blocks of mass transit? If you drive to work, you need places to park that won't eat half your paycheck. How about biking or walking? Want your gym or favorite coffee shop nearby, a grocery store on the route home, or a park close enough for a lunchtime stroll? What characteristics do you want in the community where you'll live and work? Go to the Discovery Exercise on page 40 for instructions on how to identify your ideal community.

> **66** *For each new high-tech job in a city, five additional jobs are ultimately created outside of the high-tech sector in that city. Where you live matters more than ever.* **99**

—Enrico Moretti, author of *The New Geography of Jobs*

Your Ideal Salary and Level of Responsibility

To fill in this section of your Parachute, you'll explore the level of responsibility you want, along with your level of compensation. This is the first section on your Parachute where we will be looking at two different time frames: soon, and in the future.

How much responsibility you take on will affect the ways and with whom you interact. The amount of money you want to make can strongly influence where you live. Salaries vary wildly depending on industry, geography, or supply and demand, and these realities can turn your ideal location into not-so-ideal.

A job finances your life. What level of financing do you want? You'll need to research starting salaries and wages for experienced workers. See the Parachute Tip on page 41 for recommended salary websites. Keep in mind that salary information is often very general. Career literature often quotes national averages or median salary. You need to know starting salaries for the jobs you want in the city, town, or region where you prefer to live. Double-check all compensation information with mentors or people who work in the industries, fields, or locations that most interest you.

People routinely brag about what they paid for an item, but most are secretive about what they earn (parents included). Asking people "What's your salary?" or "How much do you earn?" has been historically taboo. More recently, there is increased understanding of the connection between transparency about salaries and reducing income inequality. Check with the companies you want to work for, are their salaries published? Do research online. To get a broad idea of income, ask those you interview about typical pay for entry-level positions. If you keep your questions away from their personal earnings, people will help you get accurate salary information. You can ask a less direct question, such as "The average starting salary for this job nationally is $36,750 a year. Are local starting salaries similar?"

The ideal situation is to find high-demand jobs that you like a lot. If you make time for research, it's very likely you can find jobs in your favorite fields that pay well. If you can't, your challenge is to figure out whether it's more important to you

My Ideal Community

GEOGRAPHICAL FEATURES: DO YOU WANT TO LIVE . . .
- In or near the mountains? near the coast? in the desert? on the plains? by a river?
- In a small town (fewer than 5,000 people), a medium-sized city (5,000 to 20,000), a large city (20,000 to 500,000), or a major metropolitan area (500,000 or larger)?
- In a rural area with a town or city within a reasonable distance, or in an isolated area far from "civilization"?

PEOPLE: DO YOU PREFER . . .
- A good mix of age, ethnic, economic, and religious groups?
- Mostly people your own age or in your own ethnic, economic, or religious group?
- Living where you already have friends or family, or in a place where everyone is new?

NEIGHBORHOOD/HOUSING: DO YOU PREFER LIVING . . .
- In an apartment, condominium, or tiny house?
- In a subdivision? In a single-family home that doesn't look like everyone else's?

CULTURE: WHAT IS IMPORTANT TO YOU . . .
- Good bookstores, art galleries, libraries, and museums?
- Movie theaters? Music, dance, and the arts?
- A local semi-pro or pro sports team?

EDUCATIONAL OPPORTUNITIES: WHAT IS IMPORTANT TO YOU . . .
- Personal enrichment classes? Professional development classes?
- A college or university?

RECREATION: WHAT WOULD YOU LIKE YOUR COMMUNITY TO HAVE . . .
- Good parks? Bike paths, walking/hiking trails?
- Community sports leagues and facilities?

COMMUTING: WHAT IS IMPORTANT TO YOU . . .
- Commute by car?
- Ability to take mass transit to work?
- Being able to walk or bike to work?
- How far are you willing to drive to an airport?

Write the answers to these questions on small slips of paper or sticky notes and arrange them in order of their importance to you. Select the top five characteristics and write them in the My Ideal Community section of My Parachute (page ix). Like using an online grid? Go to www.successonyourownterms.com/prioritizing_grid.htm?items=10&.

The categories and items on this list are not your only choices. We hope these suggestions will stimulate additional ideas about what makes a community ideal for you. Don't overlook brainstorming with a group of friends to get more ideas.

to have a steady income (doing something you enjoy less) or to work in a field that absolutely fascinates you (but doesn't pay as well).

Answer the questions on page 42 to figure out your ideal salary and level of responsibility.

PARACHUTE TIP

Helpful websites for salary info:

- Glassdoor.com
- LinkedIn.com (Google how to use LinkedIn to gather salary or company info.)
- Payscale.com
- Salary.com (note that this site charges a fee for reports beyond basic information)
- Vault.com

REALITY CHECK

Teens and young adults often have unrealistic ideas about salaries. A 2020 study found recent college graduates overestimated their starting salaries by 23 percent ($58,000 expected; $47,000 actual average). Grads also overestimated their earnings ten years into their careers by $15,000 annually. Recent nonengineering graduates working in tech fields were surprised to learn that $51,000—the typical starting salary at well-known San Francisco Bay Area companies—wasn't enough to rent their own one-bedroom apartment. Don't be caught by surprise; do your salary homework for jobs in the cities where you most want to live.

My Ideal Salary

Your salary finances your life. Currently, a majority (55 percent) of young adults between the ages of 25 and 35 live with their parents. That was a trend even before the COVID-19 pandemic. If you don't want to be living in your folks's basement, you'll want to pick a job or career that pays well enough for you to have your own place, even if that place is shared with other young people.

Ask yourself:

- What salary do I want to make when I get out of school? (If you have no idea, build a budget at https://www.jumpstart.org/what-we-do/support-financial-education/reality-check/)

- What's the starting salary of the jobs I want in the area where I want to live? (Regional salaries can vary greatly from national averages.)

- What salary do I need to finance life in my twenties?

- What salary do I hope to be making after five years of experience?

- What do I want my top salary to be?

- Which of the jobs that interest me most will pay what I hope to earn?

- What does it cost to rent a room, studio, one bedroom apartment, or house in the city where I hope to live?

Research online and by contacting people familiar with the jobs or fields in which you intend to work. Which compelling jobs pay what you'd like to earn now, and in the future?

Write your rock-bottom starting salary and your ideal salary on the My Parachute diagram in the section labeled My Ideal Salary (page ix). This is your salary range. Will your ideas about salary change over time? Undoubtedly.

If your goal is to make a lot of money, pick a field that fascinates you. The late Srully Blotnick, a PhD in business psychology, wanted to know what happened to people who "go for the money." He studied the career choices and financial success of fifteen hundred people who had MBAs (Masters in Business Administration). He divided them into two groups. Group A, which contained 83 percent of the people in the study, chose careers they believed could earn them a lot of money. Group B, or 17 percent of the study group, chose careers because of their interest in the work. Who do you think made more money?

Twenty years later, 101 of the fifteen hundred had become millionaires. One hundred of those were from Group B, who made choices based on interests. Only one millionaire was from Group A, those who chose careers to make money. This research shows that *you are one hundred times more likely to be financially successful if you work in a field that fascinates you.*

My Ideal Level of Responsibility

The world of work is filled with jobs that happen at differing levels of responsibility. What level of responsibility appeals most to you? Do you want to be an employee, salesperson, supervisor, or manager? Do you want to own the place? Are you a risk taker, or an entrepreneurial type not afraid of failure? What is the "level of worry" you want to take on? If you don't want to bring your work worries home with you, choose your level carefully. You may start out at one point—entry-level supervised by others—but over time you can gain the education and experience to advance to a management level.

After thinking about what level of responsibility you want in your first career path, briefly summarize what you want below and on your My Parachute diagram (page ix).

_____

_____

_____

_____

_____

The Discovery Exercises you did in the preceding three chapters complete most of the pieces in your career puzzle. Now that all but the center is filled out and prioritized, your My Parachute diagram describes the top components of a good job fit for you. With investigation, the pieces will come together to create possibilities for your career direction.

CHAPTER 4

Your Parachute Describes Your Dream Jobs

Your Parachute describes the components of a job that will fit you. It's very hard to find something if you don't know what you're looking for. The Parachute diagram was created make it easier for you to find jobs that fit your definition of great. Once your Parachute is filled in, you have a visual composed of words—a different kind of picture. Your Parachute is a bit like the old TV show *Concentration*, which was based on a children's memory game, where images and parts of words had to be strung together to create a common saying or phrase. Luckily, your Parachute doesn't have missing sections that make it harder to guess what the clues mean.

But like *Concentration*, your Parachute may be easy or difficult to interpret. You may look at your Parachute, smack your forehead and say, "Of course!" But if you look at your Parachute and have no idea which jobs might make you happy, keep reading this chapter.

Even if your Parachute diagram confirms a career path you desire, you must still do two things: (1) talk to people doing that work, and (2) develop two more job targets. Talking to people in your chosen career, or seeking internship, apprenticeship, or job shadowing opportunities can prevent you from spending time and money preparing for work you won't like. Without feedback from people doing the work you hope to do, your career choices may be based on hearsay, or glamorized projections from movies or TV shows that don't reflect real life. Having two additional jobs or job clusters that overlap your Parachute is just good insurance, offering you the flexibility of choosing a new direction if your first or second path becomes blocked. A Parachute word picture can fit many jobs, and one never knows what the future holds. Try not to narrow your options too quickly. Humans are more comfortable with labels than puzzles, but don't lock yourself into a job title without looking at all the opportunities that combine your best skills and favorite interests—otherwise you might pass by an excellent job without realizing it!

Generally, your interests and abilities point to the fields in which you will discover jobs you'll like. Your transferable and self-management skills help lead you to jobs you'll enjoy within those fields. The remaining sections of your Parachute contain values which will help you decide between job offers.

> **66** *I wish I had known that there were opportunities to earn a comfortable living much closer to the types of dreams and interests that I had in high school. I was an avid lover of maps back then. Had I known that being a cartographer was an available career, I would have fervently pursued it.* **99**
>
> —Adam Hoverman, DO, family practice physician, age 30

Transform Interests into Fields

The process of finding potential jobs that match your Parachute will involve a little translation. Your favorite interests could easily suggest one field, or they may fit into multiple occupational fields or industries.

If skateboarding is one of your interests, fields you might consider could include athletics, recreation, kinesiology (the study of the principles of mechanics and anatomy in relation to human movement), or mechanical or materials engineering. In the field of athletics, you might become a skateboarding coach. In recreation, you might create skateboard teams or a program for new skateboarders. If you combine kinesiology with engineering, you might design skateboards that are safer and easier to maneuver. Maybe you tinkered with a skateboard for a disabled friend or relative. If that experience got you interested in adapting other recreational equipment, you might study robotics or mechanical engineering. The training and education you need varies according to the field you pick.

Here's another example: Tamara wants to be a nurse. Her top interest is medicine, and her best skills are taking care of sick or injured people. Tamara is good at math and science, especially chemistry, and her self-management skills include being calm and methodical in a crisis. The kind of nurse she becomes depends on the type of training she completes, the major she chooses, and her other interests.

While the field of medicine is quite broad, here are some of the nursing jobs Tamara could pursue:

- If she wants to work with children, she could be a pediatric nurse. In this instance, her chosen field would be pediatrics.

- If serving cancer patients is a strong interest, Tamara could be an oncology nurse. (Field = oncology)

- Tamara could be an emergency room nurse, work on a search-and-rescue team, or be part of a Life Flight medical team. (Field = emergency medicine)

- She could be a nurse on a cruise ship or at a large resort. (Field = recreation)

The same job happens in many different fields, some of which you'd like and some you'd hate!

 DISCOVERY EXERCISE

Translate Interests into Fields

1. Turn to My Parachute, page viii. Look at the section entitled My Favorite Interests.

2. Take your list of favorite interests to a reference librarian. They may make suggestions or point you to references where you can get ideas.

3. Go to Onetonline.org. Click on Advanced Search, and a drop-down menu will let you search for work using eight different factors, including interests, abilities, and skills.

4. Research until you have chosen two or three fields for each interest, and two or three jobs (or one job cluster) that you like in each of those fields.

5. List these fields somewhere on your Parachute diagram, or in a separate document or journal.

It may take a few weeks of research to find the fields that best suit your interests.

Get help from parents, school counselors, librarians, or career center staff to complete this exercise. Keep in mind that it's fine to start with guesses; your research into jobs in each field or family that interests you will help you uncover precise names for those jobs that fit you best.

If you need more help translating interests into fields, check out *Transform Interests Into Jobs*, a workbook offering step-by-step instructions for finding fields based on interests. Disclosure: I am that book's coauthor.

66 *Curiosity turns work into play.* **99**

—Paul Graham, creative techie and blogger

PARACHUTE TIP

The words "career" and "job" are often used interchangeably. You can usually determine the meaning of the word by its context. The word "job" typically refers to one position. "Career" generally refers to your total time in the world of work and involves a series of jobs in a related field. To build your first career path, you will learn about jobs, careers, and professions. As your knowledge of a career field broadens, your job goals may change.

Explore Lots of Jobs to Find a Fit

With your interests now translated into fields, it's time to find jobs in those fields that fit you best. Do you already have an idea of what those jobs may be? Great. Again, find people you can talk with about those jobs. You want to confirm that they fit your Parachute and learn what education or experience you need to get hired. If you have no clue how to solve the puzzle of your Parachute, here are steps you can take to discover jobs worth exploring:

- Show your Parachute to people whose opinions and suggestions you trust. See the next Discovery Exercise for ways to present your skills and interests. The best idea generator is a small group of people.

- Read tons of information about different occupations. Ask reference librarians or career center staff to direct you to resources that will help you find jobs that fit your skills and fields of interest.

- Industries and occupational fields have websites that give information about available jobs. Use the words "jobs in _____(fill in) industry" to search.

- Keep an eye out for jobs mentioned in magazines, blogs, or TV programs. Do any of them interest you enough to investigate?

- Find people who work or have worked in fields that intrigue you. Facebook, LinkedIn, YouTube, blogs, and podcasts can be really useful for this. Talk with new hires as well as well-established workers.

Using Your Parachute

Research has found that minds need a lot of information before making a good decision. And in order to be most useful, that information needs to be in meaningful categories and prioritized. Sounds like your Parachute diagram, right? But you can get overwhelmed by too much information. Having each section of your Parachute on a separate sheet of paper lets you examine one or two categories, and then slowly add new puzzle pieces.

1. Once all the information in your Parachute is prioritized, write the name of each category on a separate index card or half sheet of paper. If your writing is hard to read, type it up and print it from a computer. The sections of your Parachute that detail your interests and transferable and self-management skills are particularly important for the process of finding your ideal jobs.

2. First look at your interests. If you've taken an ability test, list your top three abilities along with your interests. Label this list Interests and Abilities. Write down the names of any jobs or fields that come to mind while looking at your interests and abilities.

3. Next, list your transferable and self-management skills next to your interests and abilities and read the information in each category. When you combine all three categories, do potential types of work come to mind?

4. Get job, industry, or field suggestions from other people by showing them your list of interests, abilities, transferable skills, and self-management skills. Write down all their suggestions, but only research the ones that appeal to you. Read about the jobs or fields you think match your Parachute. If a job seems to suit you, divide what you learn about it into sections similar to the way you organized your Parachute. It will make comparing the factors of a job with your Parachute much easier.

YOUR PARACHUTE — WHERE TO START YOUR RESEARCH — HIGH SKILL, HIGH DEMAND JOBS WHERE YOU WANT TO LIVE

- Most counties have a Small Business Organization with retired volunteers who have experience in running a business. They know about running a business and the jobs that happen within that business. Your county's SBO is a good place to learn about employers and learn how to write a business plan.

Career-Development Planning Tools

In addition to your Parachute, there are other career tools you need to know and put into practice. Building a network through information interviews, the Job Meter, and writing thank-you notes will all help you find and get a really cool job. You'll learn about these things in the rest of this chapter. First, let's explore gathering career information through field research.

In career exploration and job-search classes, this field research goes by many names. You'll hear it called networking, informational interviewing (quite the tongue twister), and other phrases. Essentially, it's gathering information you need for career planning by talking with people.

Network Building

The older you get, the more you'll hear the word *networking*. Not everyone understands the point of networking—some think it's collecting as many business cards or meeting as many people as they can. It's not. The goal of networking is to bring helpful people into your orbit. Network building expands your connections to people who can help you find what you seek. This group of people is called a network. You build a network by meeting people who work in your chosen field.

Career-focused networking helps you build a contact list of people in your field who can share resources and make things happen. Building networks is a tried-and-true career choice and job-search strategy. Your options for jobs, colleges, courses to take, and skills to learn are greatly enhanced by networking.

Network building can be done either informally or formally. *Informal network building* happens when you want to learn more about an issue, hobby, or activity. Have you ever asked someone where he bought his cool shoes? Or tried to find an extra ticket to a must-see concert through friends or acquaintances? If yes, then you've done informal networking.

Formal network building is more focused on gathering information about current conditions and trends in a specific job or field. Having an information interview with someone who has the job you want is an example of formal networking, and can be useful in preparing you to get ready for a job hunt or find the perfect job.

PARACHUTE TIP

Have you had many pleasant conversations with adults? Does the thought of talking to an adult about their work stress you out? Through practice information interviews, you can practice your interviewing skills to make the experience less stressful. Talking about something you enjoy isn't intimidating. What are your favorite hobbies or activities? Is there a building in town you've long wanted to visit? Pick one or two things you're so interested in or knowledgeable about that you could talk to *anyone* about them, then find someone with whom you share that interest or hobby and talk to them about it.

Make your first practice interviews with someone you know. Ask how they got interested in the topic, what they like about it, what they don't like about it, and if they know other people with the same interests. Have at least one practice interview with someone you don't know, and ask those same questions. Practice interviews will help you overcome fears of talking with strangers—something you'll do a lot in your work life.

If you do two to five of these practice interviews, you'll learn what it feels like to have a conversation about a strong interest; that's exactly what information and hiring interviews are. Once practice interviews feel comfortable, you'll be ready to do information interviews.

Getting hired is still a person-to-person activity. Whether you make your contacts through online connections or people you know personally, you'll find seven times more job opportunities via formal networking than through ads (print or online job sites). Through your network, you can . . .

- Gain a realistic view of a job from someone actually doing it every day.

- Determine if a work environment suits you.

- Meet people attracted to your ideal job or profession to see if they share your values.

- Learn industry jargon, trends, and issues. This helps you speak confidently as someone who knows the industry.

- Find mentors and leaders in the field or industry.

- Learn better, faster ways to achieve job qualifications.

- Discover how climate change, robotics, or AI could impact the work you want to do.

- Set up a Twitter account and start following both the giants and the up-and-comers in your chosen field or industry.

You will want to excel at networking, as it is a necessary tool for achieving your professional goals.

PARACHUTE TIP

Wondering if information interviews are lame, terrifying, or pointless? Get your hands on *Make Things Happen* by Lara Zielin (Lobster Press, 2003). This book is fun, easy to read, and in just one hundred pages breaks out the how and why of information interviews and network building. The book has a great explanation of Six Degrees of Separation, and how they can affect job hunting.

Information Interviews

Information interviews are opportunities for you to gather information for career decisions by talking to someone doing the job. A trusted adult—parents, parents of friends, friends of friends—can help you find people with jobs you're curious about. Other potential information interviewees can be found through professional directories, local businesses, local service clubs, or the internet. Most social networking platforms including Facebook, LinkedIn, Pinterest, Instagram, and Twitter can help you find people to connect with and interview. (See chapter 8 for details on using social media to network.)

Each person's experience with a job is different. So, before crossing a particular job or career off your list, talk to at least three people to gather the most accurate and balanced information. If you don't like what you hear about a job after talking with a few people, there's no need to spend any more time pursuing it.

You can conduct these interviews by phone, FaceTime, Zoom or other real time video platform. Interviewing people in person at their work site is even better, because you can see how their work environment compares to your ideal. Don't make career decisions without seeing several work settings.

Safety tip: Never feel that you have to go alone to an information interview—even if someone you trust made the recommendation, and especially if you're under the age of eighteen. If you can't get an interview companion, always meet at a work site during business hours, when other people are around. No closed doors. Or you can opt to have your interview by phone or video conference.

> **REALITY CHECK**
>
> For the jobs that interest you most, try to seek out the youngest people you can find in those roles. The people you will most often be referred to first are those considered to be successful in their field, and they may be fifteen to twenty years older than you. They'll have a lot of good information to share about their work, but industry changes and other factors can cause job satisfaction to vary by age group.

Information Interview FAQs

The following are common questions about setting up information interviews:

With whom do I talk? Speak with someone who has the job that interests you. If this person's supervisor is easier to find, talk with them to get connected to the jobholder. Bosses and hiring managers often have the best information about how to train for the work you want to do. But don't stop with the boss; it's important to learn about the job from an employee perspective.

Will I need an appointment? Probably. If the jobs that interest you are in locations that are open to the public, like retail stores or hotels, you may be able to walk in during a slow time and find someone who will talk with you. "What's it like to work here?" is an easy way to get someone talking.

If the job or organization you want to learn more about has limited public access, is further away, or if the person you're trying to reach is very busy, you'll need to schedule an appointment for a fifteen-to-twenty-minute conversation. You can make the appointment by phone or email.

What do I say to make an appointment? Develop a short script introducing yourself to the person you'd like to interview, known as a "pitch." Here's a sample:

> Hi, my name is Megan. My father gave me your name because you own a mobile pet-care business. I like animals very much. I'm collecting information about pet-centered businesses. Could I make an appointment to talk with you about your work? I'll need about fifteen minutes of your time.

People may want to know more about you and why you want to talk with them about their job. Be ready to answer questions about who you are, how you picked them, and why you want to talk with them.

What if I freeze on the phone? Type out your script and have it in front of you when you make calls. If you freeze, you'll be able to refer quickly to your script.

Can I contact someone first with a note? In the sales field, contacting someone you don't know is termed "a cold call." If you find cold-calling intimidating, your first contact can be in writing through snail mail or email. You'll need an exact physical or email address. Mention that you will follow up with a phone call to set up an appointment, then be sure to make that follow-up call. If you say you'll call at a specific time and date, then do! Here is a sample of a written request:

> Dear Amanda Ruiz,
>
> My name is Taneesha Jones. I am studying mechanical engineering and robotics at Tidewater College. My robotics teacher showed me an article on bionic limbs that you wrote for LiveScience.com. My ultimate career goal is to assist in creating new medical equipment so that people regain their mobility after spinal injuries. I hope to work for a year or two before transferring to a university.
>
> I know you must be very busy, but I am hoping you can spare twenty minutes to talk with me about your work. I would appreciate your suggestions as to what entry-level jobs I might qualify for and what university major might best prepare me for future jobs.
>
> If you would reply with some convenient times to phone you for an appointment, I would be very grateful.
>
> Sincerely,
> Taneesha Jones

Will someone meet with me? Yes, but not everyone, of course. If you speak courteously when requesting an appointment, communicate clearly what information you're seeking, and show gratitude for your contact's time, eight out of ten people you phone will make an appointment to see you.

People love to talk about themselves, and most of them remember being in high school and not having a clue about how to choose a career or get a job. Adults will be impressed that you're doing research now to learn about jobs that will be a good fit for you. Those who are impressed will be very helpful.

If your interviewee likes what they do and enjoys talking about it, you may find it hard to keep your appointment to its original time limit. It helps to tell your interviewees at the beginning that you have five or six questions. To keep your appointment within the agreed time, say twenty minutes, they have just four minutes per question. Should the interview run over time despite your efforts, your interviewee may invite you to stay a bit longer. Don't stay over forty minutes.

On the day of the interview be sure to dress in business casual attire, arrive a few minutes early, have your questions ready, and be prepared to take notes.

Why would someone see me? You stand out as a high school student researching career goals and that gives you the Wow factor. You are sure to hear, "Wow, I'm so impressed you're doing career research so young" or "Wow, I wish I had done this kind of career investigation when I was your age."

Do I have to go alone? No. If you're under eighteen, you shouldn't go to information interviews by yourself. If you're over eighteen, you can have a trusted adult go with you until you feel comfortable doing information interviews on your own. (Of course, this is not true of hiring interviews! A potential employer would question your self-sufficiency if you brought someone to your hiring interview.)

Consider taking a friend with you; joint information interviews are valuable if both of you want to know about the job or field. Choose someone who knows how to behave in business situations and won't embarrass you. It's good business etiquette to ask the person you're interviewing in advance if they mind an additional person joining you. Don't just show up with someone else.

What should I ask the person I'm interviewing? You should have questions as a result of your research, and new questions may come to mind during the interview. That's great! Along the way, make sure you ask the same questions at each interview for easy comparison afterward—an absolute necessity for good research.

Ask the following five questions in every information interview you do:

1. How did you get into your job? What kind of training or education did you get?

2. What are three to five tasks that you do most often? How often do you do them? What skills are necessary to perform these tasks?

3. What do you like about your job? What don't you like about your job?

4. What changes are predicted for your field over the next five to ten years?

5. Do you know anyone else I can speak with who also does this or similar work? Are you comfortable providing their contact information?

As you listen to the person's answers, take notes. You can create a form for notes with the same categories as those on your Parachute, or copy your notes later by dividing what you learned into Parachute categories.

Let's say you're interviewing Dr. Kelly, a veterinarian. In response to your question, "How did you get into your job?," she answers, "I've loved animals since I was a little kid. I always had cats, dogs, birds, horses, and all kinds of other pets. Whenever one of them got hurt, I'd calm it down, clean out the wound if it wasn't too serious, and help it heal. Math and science are my favorite subjects. I always thought it would be great to be able to help animals all the time when I grew up, so I became a veterinarian."

In her answer, Dr. Kelly told you about her interest in animals and the skills she used working with them. So in Dr. Kelly's Parachute under My Favorite Interests, you would write, "caring for animals," "math," and "science." Under My Best Transferable Skills, you'd write "calming animals and cleaning their wounds."

Later, Dr. Kelly mentions that it's important for her to work with people who are compassionate and who love animals—write that information under My Favorite Types of People. Does Dr. Kelly say why she chose to become a large-animal veterinarian? Does work with large animals keep her outside, which she loves (details for My Ideal Work Environment)? Does she live in a rural area where people work with animals for a living (that would go under My Ideal Community)?

Dividing information into your Parachute categories makes comparisons easy. Where does your Parachute overlap with hers? Where does it differ?

To students just starting build their networks, the most important question to ask is the last one: "Do you know anyone else I can speak with who also does this or similar work?" Dr. Kelly might give you the name of a veterinarian who works with small animals, cares for animals at a zoo or a racetrack, or works as a veterinary surgical technician. Each name is an additional contact. If you receive two or three names from each person you interview, you'll soon have a huge network for learning about jobs you might like. Treat your networking contacts well, and they could help you with a job search later.

The Job Meter

It doesn't make sense to interview additional people if it's clear you are no longer interested in the work they do. Let's say that after interviewing Dr. Kelly and another veterinarian, you decide that seven years of higher education is not for you. If a couple of years of education sounds perfect and your math and science grades are good, starting your career as a veterinary technician may be very appealing. There are many kinds of veterinary technicians. You interview three technicians in four different subspecialties. Voilà! You find a great match and make a decision.

If, after an information interview or two, you know that a particular career doesn't float your boat, how do you find people whose work suits you better? The Job Meter can help you formulate questions that will lead you to jobs that match your Parachute better.

The Job Meter is the creation of Marty Nemko, PhD, a brilliant, creative career consultant and author (www.martynemko.com). The Job Meter helps you construct questions that uncover work that is closer to your Parachute. Here's how:

1. Listen to someone describing their job. Compare it to your Parachute and your hopes. Give the job a rating on a scale of 1 to 10 (1 = awful; 10 = perfect).

2. For ratings lower than 8.5, ask yourself, "What would have to be different about this job in order for it to be a 10?"

3. At the end of your interview, describe how the job of your dreams differs from their job. Remember, your interviewee does this work every day, so don't say things like, "Your job sounds really awful!" or "I'd hate to do this work!" Instead, describe the qualities you'd prefer. If you want less contact with people and more use of your estimating skills, you would ask your interviewee to name jobs with those features. Do they have ideas for you? Are they willing to share contacts with you, or use their name to open more doors? Remember, people's professional contacts are part of their net worth. Handle them like treasure.

4. As you perform more interviews, keep ranking, describing, and adjusting until you have a cache of jobs that are a perfect fit for you.

JOB METER STORY

Eric is seventeen. Last week he did an information interview with Steve, a stockbroker.

Eric gave that job a rank of 3 on his Job Meter. It did involve math, information analysis, and using numbers as a reasoning tool—Eric's favorite skills. On the negative side, Steve worked in a high-rise building downtown in a very formal work environment, and his colleagues—who looked stressed-out—worked in tiny cubicles. None of this appealed to Eric.

Today Eric is meeting with his mom's cousin Leah. She's barely thirty and has her own small business as a certified public accountant (CPA). She works in an old house that's been converted into office suites. The surrounding neighborhood has big, leafy trees and outdoor cafés. Leah's workplace feels much more comfortable to Eric than the stockbroker's office. After listening to Leah describe what she does, Eric told Leah about the Job Meter. Eric asked Leah what rating she'd give her job.

"A 9.9," she answered. "How would you rate my job?"

Eric hesitated, "Maybe a 5 or 6. My teacher said an 8 is the lowest number for a career target."

Luckily, Leah wasn't insulted. She smiled and asked, "For you to give it a 10, how would my job have to be different?"

"I'm not sure I want to have my own business or lots of people as clients. I'd like to use my math skills to gather information and write reports that would go to a boss or one client. Tax season seems like doing one report per client. Both you and Steve, the stockbroker I interviewed last week, spend a lot of time meeting new people. I guess that's to expand your business?"

"Yes. I belong to a service club, a community business group, and a women's professional organization. I review the annual taxes for the preschool my son goes to, and I've volunteered to be the treasurer for the co-op kindergarten he'll attend next year. I like to think I'm more subtle than wearing a button that says, 'I'm a CPA and I need your business,' but I'm constantly looking for ways to meet people who may need my services."

"I don't think I'd like constantly meeting new people," Eric said before adding, "I'd also like my day to be split between working inside and outdoors."

Leah thought for a while, then said, "I've got clients who do all kinds of different jobs. Give me a week. I need to check with them to ask if I can give you their names. I'll find people for you to talk with about careers that use math."

"Thanks, Leah. I appreciate your help," Eric responded. After the interview, Eric followed up by sending Leah a thank-you note.

Writing a Thank-You Note

After each information interview, always send a thank-you note. Why?

When you meet with people or interview them about their work, they are giving you a valuable, but limited, resource: their time. By sharing their work experience with you, they have given you career information, perhaps even wisdom or a new contact. Information that uncovers a job fit or keeps you from making an inappropriate career decision is a valuable gift, and a gift deserves to be acknowledged—especially when it's something you asked for! The people you interview will appreciate being thanked for their time, and those you have thanked may be inclined to help you again. Here are some of the considerations for keeping new contacts:

- Would you want this person to be one of your career mentors?

- Is this a job or field you'd like to explore further?

- Might you want to ask this person more questions in the future?

- Might you like to try job shadowing or interning there?

- Will you need letters of recommendation for your job search?

Get your interviewee's business card. If a receptionist, administrative assistant, or other gatekeeper was helpful or encouraging, get their business card as well and send them a thank-you note. Writing a thank-you note over email just takes seconds but makes you unforgetable!

Does your interviewee not have a business card? Be sure to write down their contact details at the beginning of your interview. Ask for their job title, business address, the correct spelling of names, and email. Send a note of appreciation to every person you interview, even if you are not in love with the work they do. You never know whom you might cross paths with again, and who could end up being helpful down the line.

PARACHUTE TIP

Email or snail mail? Thank-you notes typed or handwritten? These used to be hotly debated. Email is the preferred method of business communication; it's quicker, easier to spell check, and less likely to get lost. If someone doesn't have email, then use USPS. Don't text unless that's what your interviewee prefers (you know this because you asked them!). Texting is a tad informal and can be intrusive into someone's workday.

Thank-You Note Tips

After you leave the interview, make an outline of what you appreciated or learned while it's still fresh in your mind. Three tips while writing your note:

1. Keep it simple. A thank-you note can be just two or three sentences.

2. Proofread and spell-check a bazillion times to avoid errors that could make you look unprofessional.

3. Send right away. A thank-you note that arrives a week later seems like an afterthought, not genuine gratitude.

Here's a sample thank-you note:

Dear Mr./Ms./Mx./Dr. _____ :

Thank you for talking with me this morning about your work. The information you gave me about work/study and apprenticeship programs is very helpful. I very much appreciate that you were willing to take the time to meet with me.

If I have further questions, may I contact you again? If you are too busy but could refer me to a colleague, I would be most grateful.

Sincerely,
Your Name

PARACHUTE TIP

People appreciate thank-you notes, and getting one can totally make someone's day.

No matter what form of thank-you note, be sure to:

- Use standard English (don't write in all caps or all lowercase).
- Use proper punctuation and grammar (no run-on or stream-of-consciousness sentences).
- Run spell-check tools multiple times.
- Ask a friend who geeks out on grammar or an adult to proof-read your first notes. Spell-check is helpful, but your eyes and brain can be fooled.

DO YOU NEED A CAREER COACH?

Career coaching can help high school students learn more about the types of jobs they would like to prepare for, or college majors they might pursue. A coach can guide you through discovering your marketable skills, identifying your fields of fascination, and determining viable post–high school options faster than you can working by yourself. A coach will carefully listen to your wants, needs, and goals. During coaching sessions, the coach will use questions, written exercises, and feedback to help you make informed decisions about your first career path. To learn more about what a career coach can do, visit www.youthleadershipcareers.com.

And Then . . .

When you've discovered three to five jobs that hit high on your Job Meter, make a prioritized list. File it in hard copy or on your computer with your other job-search materials.

To gather that list of three to five jobs that fascinate you, expect to do four to six hours of online research, and ten to twenty-five information interviews. If you've done twenty-five information interviews and don't have a list of jobs that fill your occupational dreams, either your Parachute doesn't truly reflect what you want, or your career choices aren't making *you* happy. This is a clue that it's time to give some deeper thought to what you really want for your future.

If more than nine months have gone by since your last job search, review your Parachute. Update the sections to reflect your recent experience. An up-to-date Parachute helps you find more satisfying options for summer jobs, internships, part-time work, and courses of study.

Do you see why it's recommended that you begin career planning early in high school? You will most likely have more time in high school for career exploration than you will ever have again. You have many contacts through school—from favorite teachers, to booster clubs, to local employers that you won't have easy access to once you leave high school. Remember your *Wow* factor: adults will open lots of doors for ambitious high school students.

Kudos for getting this far! We hope you've discovered some things about yourself that you didn't know, and confirmed other things you did know.

The discoveries you've made about yourself in Part One will guide your search for your first career job. Effective job-search techniques are presented in Part Three.

But first, in Part Two we'll look at getting the most out of high school and college, and other tools that can get you further down the road toward finding the career that's right for you.

What If My Ideal Job Is Working for Myself?

One-third of the workforce is self-employed, and not always by choice. In any job market, fair or foul, you need to know what kind of business you could start that would give you an income stream quickly. Mega-entrepreneur Richard Branson suggests that if you make a list of the things you love and the things that irritate you, ideas for products or services exist in both. The internet has been a boon for young entrepreneurs. There are more Millennial and Gen Z entrepreneurs than in previous generations.

You may like to tinker, have an idea for how to make something better, or want to provide a service that is needed in your community. People who set up their own businesses for profit are called *entrepreneurs*. People who establish a nonprofit to provide services to a special population or target a special issue are called *social entrepreneurs*.

Entrepreneurial and social entrepreneur wannabes can find related articles, blogs, associations, summer camps, competitions, and success stories in books and online. While you are living at home is a great time to create your own business, like the eleven- and nine-year-old brothers who created a math game app for iPhones. Write a brief business plan. Research how you would start and grow a business. Guy Kawasaki's book the *Art of the Start* is an excellent guide to starting a business.

❝ *There's no one clear path to your ideal job. Have as many experiences as you can; take advantage of every opportunity. Start in high school. Don't be afraid of that bad job or difficult manager, the boring class or uncomfortable field trip. Each experience, each bad fit gives you more self-awareness. By knowing yourself you learn to leverage everything you've got for everything you want.* **❞**

—Dan Schawbel, author of *Me 2.0: 4 Steps to Building Your Future*

PART TWO

On the Way to Your Future

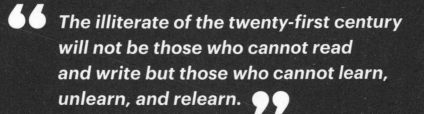 The illiterate of the twenty-first century will not be those who cannot read and write but those who cannot learn, unlearn, and relearn.

—Alvin Toffler

Does it seem that the future is far away? Look back to your life two years ago. Does it feel like those two years went by quickly? Two years from now you may be halfway through high school or even graduating. Does finding work you love to do seem like a fantasy? If you spend your high school years taking steps to turn your dreams into reality, it will happen. Right now—this moment, this week, this year—you are creating your future.

Chapter 5 covers ways to make the most of your high school to get closer to your ideal first career. Chapter 6 summarizes your options for higher education to prepare for work you'll love, and includes higher education options for all kinds of learners. Chapter 7 is about setting and achieving your goals—the tools that will help shape your future *and* get you through this school year! Chapter 8 is a new spin on an old tool: using social media sites for career exploration and job search.

Consciously using your high school and college years to learn the basics of career development will give you the skills to convert your hopes for life and work into reality.

66 *The power of vision is extraordinary.* **99**

—Dewitt Jones, award-winning *National Geographic* photographer

CHAPTER 5

What Do I Do Now? Make the Most of High School

A survey of working adults reported that their number one regret was that they did not spend enough time researching and creating options for education, jobs, and life after high school.

No need for you to have similar regrets. As you enter and move through high school, think out what you want to do in high school and what you want high school to do for you. You might want to:

- Explore your abilities with languages, music, science, art, sports, or leadership.

- Pursue an apprenticeship, an internship with a local employer, or the military.

- Research a new career or job every week until you know three that fit your Parachute and your pocketbook.

- Get ready for college.

- Learn enough skills to support yourself after graduation so you can take a break from being a student for a while.

- Gain expertise to find a fun job to finance your life while you figure out your next career path.

- Make time to explore each and every job or career that interests you.

- Become fluent in a language and use your new skills to travel.

Once you know what you most want to fit into your schedule while in high school, it's much easier to make year-by-year plans to achieve your goals. You can always add to your goals or change them as you go along. Starting out with a focus for your time in high school ensures that you won't just float along and later regret missed opportunities.

Students know that to succeed, they need reasonably good grades. Adults look to this as a sign of academic maturity. But most students don't know the importance of *career* maturity. Career maturity means you know enough about yourself and the world of work to make achievable plans for life after high school. Both types of maturity are necessary for college and career readiness.

Strategic planning is what successful businesses do. Once a company knows its goals, it can develop strategy and allocate resources to achieve those goals. Successful individuals do strategic planning too. Your Parachute diagram can help you develop a detailed plan to achieve the job and life you want in your twenties. But just a plan isn't enough; you must research your plan thoroughly. You can do this by yourself, but you'll probably get better information if adults help you.

A detailed plan? Really? Studies of young adults show that those who achieve life and career ambitions had a detailed plan whether they continued on to higher education or not. In high school, a plan reminds students why they are in school and how their classes relate to their future. When obstacles arise (and they will), students with plans create strategies for overcoming them, rather than giving up. Successful adults also have a Plan B. Life isn't always predictable—that's why this book encourages you to create not only options for your first career choice, but a second and third as well.

Does getting a job or starting a career seem light years away? It's not. The future always arrives faster than we expect! Without help or planning, transitioning from high school to your preferred career can take years—even decades. Start work on this transition while you're still in high school, and you'll be in a good job by the time you're twenty-five. Your high school classes and extracurricular activities can build a strong base for your first career pathway.

Use your high school years to set up a campaign that will help you achieve your future career goals. This campaign includes increasing your awareness of the work world, developing job-search skills, and learning which higher education options are affordable and can help you achieve your first career goals. And because it's good to think about what lies ahead, we'll also start looking at what comes after high school.

PARACHUTE TIP

In the United States, young people are eligible for hire with a work permit starting at age thirteen. If your high school has a work experience coordinator, see this person to apply for a work permit. Some businesses won't hire people under eighteen years of age without one.

Awareness of the Work World

Developing a work history is an important step to obtaining your occupational goals. Employers want to know you can show up, take instructions, and get along with coworkers and managers. Since the 1950s, teens' first jobs have often been in retail or food service. If you live in an area where there are few retail or restaurant jobs, you're going to have to get more creative in finding those first jobs to establish your work history. Many teens don't have the sophisticated knowledge skills needed for even entry-level jobs in their favorite fields. After all, that's one reason you are still in school. Your transferable skills and self-management skills may be what convinces an employer to hire you.

If you live in an area with limited first job options, find places you can volunteer. A combination of single-day events, six-month, and multiyear volunteer positions can help you establish a work history—and through those experiences you may get leads to paying jobs.

During your first two years in high school, learn the names of six jobs in your three favorite fields. In your remaining two years, study jobs in depth using the tools in this book. How well does each fit your Parachute? All the work you've done in the preceding chapters—exploring your interests, skills, and preferences concerning work environments, and identifying jobs that fit you best—increases your awareness of the job market. It's depressing how many people make career decisions without knowing the job market.

Even without realizing it, you're probably already doing things that are helping your awareness grow. You may, for example, be paying more attention to how people earn a living. You may have taken a career interest assessment that suggests some jobs you might like, but you didn't know existed. You may have older friends or siblings who have left school and started jobs with titles that are new to you. You may notice how people who enjoy their work talk about it, and compare it to those who don't enjoy their work. You may even start regularly asking adults what they do and how well they like it.

You can also increase your awareness of the work world through high school experiences, including class assignments, extracurricular activities, and part-time or summer work.

 In high school, I wish I'd known there were more options beyond doctor, lawyer, or businessperson. I also wish I'd known that you never have to choose what you are going to do forever. You can always change.

—Alice Prager, marketing manager, age 29

PARACHUTE TIP

Remember that you always have options. Is the education for your favorite job going to take too long or be too pricey? A different but related job with shorter or less expensive training might be a better option for your first career. Don't mind a year or two of further study after high school but don't like the idea of four to six years? Check out technician jobs in fields or industries that interest you. There are dozens of technician-level jobs with salaries that exceed those offered for roles requiring bachelor's degrees. One-third of community college graduates make more than the average college grad.

Class Assignments

Need to do a book report? Read a book about a superstar in the industry that most interests you, or choose a book on the basics of career development. Does some part of career development mystify you? Study it. Is someone famous for being a flaming failure? Knowing how and why someone failed can give you important tips for success. Your local bookseller or school librarian will have lots of titles for you to consider.

Need to write a research paper? Pick a profession, field, industry, or invention that fascinates you. You could research Fortune 500 companies started by people who didn't finish college. Can you find people with disabilities (such as autism, dyslexia, or ADHD) who have become famous or successful in their field?

Just assigned a history report, and you love fashion? Report on the dress and fabric of a particular historical period. Or, check out the history of a job you like. When did that kind of work start? How has it been done over a two- or three-hundred-year period?

Need to do an in-class presentation? Talk about what you learned in preparing your Parachute and conducting information interviews. Presenting your Parachute not only fulfills a class requirement but may also help your friends and classmates learn why career exploration is important for them too.

Taking a business class? Keeping track of a few stocks of publicly traded companies? Get a financial prospectus and annual reports from a couple of those companies. Ask your business teacher to help you understand and get comfortable reading those kinds of documents. Eventually, when you have the qualifications for the job you want and begin a campaign to get hired, reading the annual report of companies you want to work for gives you all kinds of good information for hiring interviews.

Does your school have a community-service requirement for graduation? Look for ways in which you can serve your community and explore your career interests at the same time. Want to be a teacher? Volunteer at a learning-oriented nonprofit. Is politics your thing? Work with the Registrar of Voters to set up a program to register students who have turned eighteen.

Extracurricular Activities

Besides being fun and a great way to make friends, extracurricular activities can help you explore career possibilities and develop valuable skills. Band, choir, drama, tutoring, peer counseling, sports, service- or interest-based clubs, student government, and dozens of other school activities can provide opportunities to test interests, hone skills, and meet new people.

If you think you'd like to teach music, investigate creating your own summer business teaching music to younger students. Or perhaps your band or choir director will let you rehearse a new piece of music with the freshman choir or band. Exploring accounting? The responsibilities as treasurer of a club allow you to track income and expenditures, create a budget, collect dues, and so on. Serving as an officer of a club, a class, or the student body will help you develop leadership and people skills, both of which can make you stand out to employers. Love drama? Write a play or musical about career-choice issues and present it to parents or to students in elementary or middle school.

Does your extracurricular activity have a particularly supportive and encouraging teacher, club adviser, band or choir director, coach, or other faculty member? Talk with them to find out how they can help you uncover jobs related to that activity, and what skills you can develop now that would be valuable in that field.

Part-Time or Summer Work

Getting conflicting messages about whether you should work while you're in high school? Economist Steve Hamilton is among those who believe that teens should focus on their studies and get good grades. According to Dr. Hamilton, "Students get more long-term benefit from improving their grades than they do from a job at Arby's. Employers are looking for signals that a young person is motivated and ambitious. Grades are one signal." If you're hoping for a merit or financial scholarship, this is particularly true.

But business owners believe having part-time or summer work during high school will help you develop important work-ethic, time-management, social, and job skills as well as a sense of responsibility. Managers for internships, apprenticeships, and jobs in your chosen field may not want to hire you without a work history. If you've got your eye on a particular internship or apprenticeship, find out a year or so before you apply if a work history will make you a stronger candidate. GPA no longer makes top-ten lists of what employers want (although dip below 2.8 at your peril!).

Perhaps family finances require that you work while in high school. Keep in mind that any job can be used to develop skills that will make you more employable down the line. Evaluate part-time jobs based on how they can train you for better jobs. Work in fast food? You gain valuable skills in working with the public. If you have a good supervisor, ask him or her to teach you some basic supervision skills. Interested in child development? A job at a child-care center will help you learn about that field. Can you get an entry-level job in a field that fascinates you? Through research and meeting people who work in that field, it could happen!

Here's some advice to etch in stone: save at least half of each paycheck. No kidding. Teenagers typically spend 98 percent of what they earn. Saving a few thousand dollars from high school jobs means you'll have money for necessary tools, lab fees, college textbooks, or a trip to check out a potential school, employer, or professional conference (where you can meet dozens of people who do the work that interests you).

Savvy Academic Choices

In high school, you must meet certain academic requirements to graduate, but you do have freedom to choose your electives. Making savvy academic choices now can help you land your perfect job later. Think you'll be going to college? Check with your college adviser or the catalog for the school that interests you. Schedule high school courses that will be most beneficial to you when you get to college. For example, certain advanced placement (AP), language, or technical courses may fulfill college requirements, enabling you to begin work on your major earlier and finish college sooner.

What if you're not certain about your future? Here are some ideas to help you no matter what you decide to do after high school:

- Keep your grades up. Strive to get the best grades you can. With each report card, ask yourself, "Did I do the best I could in every class?" If your answer isn't yes, boost your efforts.

- Is one of your goals in life to get a well-paying job? Take as many math and science classes as you can. Challenging careers and high-paying jobs often rely heavily on math and science. There is a direct correlation between level of mathematics achievement and earning power, especially for young women. If your school lacks good teachers in science or math, find a tutor or local class, go online get help through an app, or read self-help math books. A librarian or knowledgeable bookstore salesperson can give you suggestions for popular, easy-to-use books that build math skills.

- Language skills are very valuable. In addition to English, the languages of choice in the business world are Spanish and Mandarin Chinese. Want to work in a specific country? Challenge yourself to master that language while in high school. It's well known that the younger you are, the easier it is to learn a new language.

- Broaden your horizons. Learn more about your community, your country, and the world. Through your place of worship, a community-service organization, or a nonprofit agency, you may be able to find volunteer projects in your home country or abroad. Young adults with work or study abroad experience have higher starting salaries.

- Talk to adults you know and respect. How did they come to do what they're doing? Find out what they like and don't like about their work. What tips do they have for you? What do they wish they'd known earlier?

REALITY CHECK

Fewer than half of those who start university finish their degrees. Less than a third of those who go to community college graduate. Check out all options for gaining the preparation necessary for the work you want to do. These might include short-term (two months or less) certificates through online or in-person learning. In addition to manufacturing and building trade apprenticeships, earn-as-you-learn opportunities are popping up in high tech and finance. (More about these later in this chapter.)

Develop Job-Search Skills

Get good at job hunting, as you'll be using those skills often. Millennials and Gen Z are likely to have more than a dozen jobs in two or three fields. The ability to get a job in any market is a survival skill. You've already started gaining job-search skills by doing the exercises in this book. We covered basic job-hunting techniques in chapter 4; chapters 9 and 10 add more detail to these basics and introduce new techniques.

Throughout your life, you'll need to keep honing your job-search skills. Effective job-search skills can help you land an internship or a good part-time job or summer job while you're in high school. Luckily, as your skills develop, the job search becomes easier because you get more efficient and better at it.

PARACHUTE TIP

The *wow* factor: you've got it, so use it. As a teen investigating your first career path, you'll find most adults are helpful and supportive. The adults you meet doing information interviews will be amazed that you aren't waiting until after you graduate to find your career fit. They will say, "Wow! I wish I'd done this at your age."

Job searching is an interpersonal experience. Go out and talk with employers in your city, town, or county who hire for the job that interests you. If you want to live where you grew up, knowing local employers is an absolute necessity. Even if you want to move, do the research from where you live now. Local employers may be able to connect you with employers where you want to live. If you are polite and prompt in your meetings and phone calls, and send thank-you notes, adults will likely bend over backward to help you.

Here are a few activities to help increase your awareness of jobs that fascinate you and develop your job-search skills:

- Listen to guest speakers. Ask them questions. What first jobs did they get in their field? What do they look for in new hires? What classes should you take to put you on the right track?

- Listen to podcasts. Stellar people from so many different fields have done them. If someone impresses you, send them an email and tell them so.

- Explore jobs. Attend career days, visit friends or relatives in job settings, develop new contacts and conduct information interviews, get involved in volunteer work.

- You can use most social media platforms to research careers. Type the name of a job, field, or organization into the "Find friends" box on Facebook. You'll find people in your area and all around the country from whom you can learn more. Always remember to use internet safety precautions.

- Go to local conferences or meetings of professional organizations. Membership officers can tell you when the meetings are and whether you can come as a guest. As a teen, you may be able to attend conferences for free. If you're shy about going to a professional meeting or conference on your own, attend with a parent, teacher, or other adult you trust. A friend can also come along for moral support; choose someone who will help you make a good first impression.

- Read articles in journals (online or print) or magazines that deal with your future career. If you find the articles interesting, even if they're a little above your understanding, you are on a good track. Have questions? Get in touch with authors of the articles. This expands your career network. If you can't bring yourself to read the publications of your future field or industry, that may be a sign you've not chosen a career path you'll really enjoy.

- In all of your explorations, be respectful in your questions. Listen closely to answers. Ask for referrals. Send thank-you notes. Do this, and you'll receive lots of helpful suggestions from people you contact and meet.

66 *Visited an In-N-Out Burger restaurant lately? Every member of the team is fully engaged and treats customers with courtesy. I'm hiring someone that has those skills. I won't fret too much about their GPA.* **99**

—Jim Aschwanden, rancher and executive director,
California Agricultural Teachers' Association

Job Shadowing

Do you try on lots of outfits before choosing what to buy? Job shadowing lets you try on lots of jobs before you spend a dime on higher education.

Job shadowing is following a person in a particular job for a day, giving you a real feel for the day-to-day reality of specific work. Both job shadowing and on-site information interviews offer firsthand experience in real work environments to help you decide if they are a good fit for you. Does your high school have after-school career exploration or job shadow programs? If so, sign up with a friend to make the experience feel less scary.

Workplace visits show the job in 3D and can be very compelling. Try not to make any learning or education commitments until you've seen the workplaces of at least three jobs that interest you. Otherwise, how would you know if you've shadowed someone whose job is not typical? You'll get a better idea of what "normal" is by shadowing multiple people.

Job shadowing can be either informal or formal. Informal shadowing might be done with a parent, boss, or someone you've interviewed for career information, and might last two to four hours. Enthusiastic about a job? Ask for a half day. Want more time? Additional time can be scheduled on another day at your host's convenience, or your host may have suggestions for someone else to shadow. Two things are true: First, shadowing someone for eight hours takes a lot of organization and effort on their part. Your host may have to set aside certain work activities or tasks that wouldn't be appropriate to share with you. Second, you really need to know what a full eight-hour workday entails. There are jobs you could do for a couple hours a day that you absolutely could not do for eight.

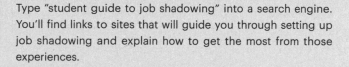

PARACHUTE TIP

Type "student guide to job shadowing" into a search engine. You'll find links to sites that will guide you through setting up job shadowing and explain how to get the most from those experiences.

Formal job shadowing is usually set up through a school, career center, or other organization. Many businesses, schools, professional organizations, agencies, and institutions use Groundhog Day, February 2, to sponsor formal job shadowing. Start early: Halloween or Thanksgiving is a good time to start checking with your school to see what job-shadowing experiences will be available in your community as part of this national program. If no one in your school knows about this, call your local chamber of commerce. If you're good at organizing and want to show initiative, another option is to set up your own informal program or start a Job-Shadowing Club at your school.

REALITY CHECK

Afraid you'll be stuck with your very first job choice? Don't worry—the US job market is changing too fast to expect a first career to last throughout your work life. The US Bureau of Labor Statistics predicts that your generation will have an average of eighteen jobs in at least two fields spanning a fifty-year career. While career arcs range from five to fifteen years, your focus right now is on your first career—not one that lasts a lifetime.

Groundhog Day programs are a good introduction, but once a year isn't enough. Freshmen should schedule at least three job-shadowing events per year; sophomores, five; juniors, seven; and seniors, nine. Summers, when workplaces are often less formal, are a good time to pursue job shadowing.

In addition to giving a firsthand look at jobs that might match your Parachute, job shadowing can help you find mentors. Mentors are so helpful that you may want more than one. Mentors can help you recognize and develop your most valuable skills in a particular field, and give you guidance on the education or training you'll need. They can link you to contacts for summer employment in your field while you're going to school and help you land a full-time job when you're ready. Mentors can give you references for job hunting and continue to guide you on the job. A good mentor is invaluable; they can share experience, wisdom, insight, and practical knowledge that you won't learn in school. You can formally ask someone to be your mentor and reach out to them every now and then when you need help. Every time your mentor spends time with you, be sure to follow up with a thank-you note.

There are national, state, and local mentoring programs. Local programs are easiest to find. Check with your school's career center, academic and club advisers, and your teachers. Your local chamber of commerce may sponsor or know of mentoring programs. Nearby community colleges and universities have mentoring programs that focus on a particular field, and offer support for getting into and completing higher education.

National mentor programs are usually connected with a field or industry. The greatest number of mentoring programs are in tech. Here are some programs to look into:

- Interested in becoming a chef? Find a mentor at http://www.acfcfc.com/about-us-2/chef-mentor-program/

- Eleventh and twelfth grade students from underrepresented populations that are interested in the sciences can find research and training opportunities through https://www.niddk.nih.gov/research-funding/research-programs/diversity-programs/research-training-opportunities-students/short-term-research-experience-underrepresented-persons-step-up

- The National Girls Collaborative Project lists over a dozen mentoring programs, including options for young women with disabilities. https://ngcproject.org/role-models-and-mentoring

- UCodeGirl is a national mentoring program that works to find local mentors for girls and teens interested in STEM careers. https://www.ucodegirl.org/stemmentorship

- Teens who identify as Black, indigenous, or people of color (BIPOC) and have interest in a publishing career can find mentors at Representation Matters Mentorship Program. https://repmatters.org/

Internships

Why is there so much buzz about internships? Employers like to hire young adults who have had one but preferably more. Why? If other factors are equal, employers hire the person they think will become productive faster than other applicants. Multiple internships show initiative and signal an applicant's ability to become productive quickly with the least training. Without several internships, many grads with bachelor's degrees in certain fields find it tough to get hired.

High school internships provide practical experience in a supervised setting. An internship might span weeks or months, depending on how long it takes to learn specific skills or procedures. Internships at the high school level are usually unpaid, although you can earn credit toward graduation. There are summer programs that do provide salaries or stipends, but internships aren't about money; they're about teaching valuable skills to make you more employable and providing firsthand information to help you make sound decisions about your career goals. If you do well, internships help you gain business contacts and employment references. Stay in touch with people you meet through internships; one of them may want to hire you once you've gotten more education or training.

Your high school guidance counselor or career center may know about formal internship programs. Adult members of your school's booster or local service clubs may also help you find an internship. Your local chamber of commerce may sponsor internships with local businesses, or they might help you set one up.

With the help of a parent, teacher, or school adviser, you can set up your own internship. Search "creating my own internship" online for more guidance. Identify a local business or agency where you'd like to work. Meet with the owner or the department manager and ask if they're willing to let you be an intern. An internship proposal should be in writing and specify the skills to be learned, the duration of the internship, the days and hours you need to be present, and who will supervise you during your internship. Writing up this proposal is a collaborative effort between you and your internship supervisor.

Employers think of internships as jobs, and you should too. If you're lucky enough to get one, show up on time and be willing to learn every day.

Data Knowledge Apprenticeships: A New Collar

You may know about apprenticeship programs in manufacturing and building trades. But do you know about the growing number of learn-and-earn opportunities, aka apprenticeships, for high school students in data knowledge? In a data knowledge apprenticeship, students work at a business a few days a week and continue their education on other days. You can find an overview to apprenticeships and how to apply at: https://www.thebalancecareers.com/best-apprenticeship-programs-5080350.

Engineering, finance, insurance, high tech, and other companies that intensely use digital data have decided they want to create and control sources for skilled employees. Tech giant IBM calls them "new collar jobs." IBM has twenty-four different data knowledge apprenticeship programs, some of which hire high school juniors and seniors, no university degree necessary. (https://www.ibm.com/us-en/employment/newcollar/apprenticeships/)

Siemens has engineering apprenticeships where students work four days a week with a supervisor who also serves as their instructor one day a week at a local community college. These engineers-in-training receive free associate's degrees and payment of about $35,000. Once a student gets their associate's degree, Siemens may pay for a bachelor's degree for those wanting to pursue further education.

Why would businesses do this? For the last thirty years, secondary education has focused on university admittance as the primary goal of high school graduates. This policy has undermined young people's ability to develop marketable skills during their four years of high school. In addition, corporations and tech businesses have grown weary of waiting the four to six years it takes to complete a bachelor's degree. Onboarding—the process of making a new hire productive—takes between ninety days and six months. From there, a new hire may quit after realizing the company isn't the right fit. New apprentice hires, meanwhile, usually work in the same department where they received their apprenticeship. They know the company we. and have had years to decide if they want to work there full time. And because they also already know how their department manager wants things done, they are productive from the moment they are hired.

Typical salaries for knowledge apprenticeships are $32,000 to $35,000 for high school students. After graduating from high school, average salaries for employees working full time after completing an apprenticeship can start at $51,000 and go as high as $75,000. In Germany and Switzerland, 70 percent of high school students have apprenticeships. That means they are self-supporting as soon as they graduate from high school.

At the time this book went to press, students in California, Colorado, Iowa, Kentucky, Maryland, Michigan, New York, North and South Carolina, Virginia, Washington, and Wisconsin have access to both blue collar and new collar apprenticeships while in high school. An online search will lead to sites and articles about apprenticeships for older teens. Does your state have earn-and-learn opportunities for high school students? Soon you may be able to go from high school to PhD through apprenticeship programs. Check with your school's career center or guidance counselor to find apprenticeships in your area. You can also check out: https://sites.ed.gov/octae/2016/11/18/apprenticeshipworks-for-high-school/

Develop a Plan

"I'm going to college or trade school" is not a plan. It's a statement. It's an idea. It might not be a good idea. A one-choice plan is like a one-legged stool: it's going to let you down!

A multipart plan lets you compare options for your best post–high school life. What interests and abilities did you list on your Parachute? Those interests and abilities lead to jobs in certain fields. What is the one subject area, field, or industry in which you would *most* like to work? Begin your plan by answering the questions below (it's likely you'll need time to do additional research):

1. Are there any entry-level jobs I can get in my favorite field with only a high school diploma? What are the starting salaries for these jobs? What would I earn in five years?

2. What jobs could I get in my favorite field with a certificate, badge, or two years (or less) of training or education? How much would it cost? What are the starting salaries for those jobs? What would I make with five years of experience?

3. Would three or four years of technical training qualify me for even better jobs in my favorite field? What are those jobs? How much would it cost? What are the starting salaries for those jobs? What would I make with five years of experience?

4. With a bachelor's degree in my favorite field, what jobs could I do? How long would that take? (Don't assume you'll get a bachelor's degree in four years; nearly 60 percent of those who get them take six years to do so.) How much would it cost? What are the starting salaries for those jobs?

5. To reach my ultimate career goal, do I need an advanced degree? What jobs would I qualify for with an advanced degree? How long would it take to get? How much would it cost? What are the starting salaries for those jobs? What would I make with more experience?

Once you accumulate this information, you need to know the following: What financial resources do you or your family have; and what amount could be borrowed, for how long, and at what interest rate? Compare the potential starting salaries for each job that interests you with the amount of money required to become qualified for those jobs. Will you earn enough for loan repayment? Gather all the answers into a one-page chart for easy comparison—Excel is a good program for creating this kind of chart—then decide which choice gives you the most bang for your educational buck.

By the start of your senior year, have your five-part plan completed (if you're the thorough type, make a five-part plan for each of your favorite fields or abilities). With current research, your higher education planning won't be a dart game! Your multipart plan gives you cost-to-earning details you can use to make choices and design a successful strategy for life after high school.

Become Financially Literate

Financial literacy means you have the skills and knowledge to make informed and effective decisions with money. Financial literacy and career planning are sort of cousins. The money you need comes from your job, which pays you a salary that supports your lifestyle. No matter what your salary is, you need to know how to conserve it so you can pay your bills and save for future needs. Not all high schools and colleges teach financial literacy. If yours does, wonderful; but if not, educate yourself. With the internet, it's easy.

Here are the top financial concepts you should learn before you graduate high school.

- **BUDGETING:** How to create and use a budget.

- **CREDIT CARDS, CREDIT, AND CREDIT SCORES:** Credit card companies will court you after you turn eighteen. Learn how to use credit cards. Unpaid credit card debt is expensive.

- **SAVINGS:** Save a portion of everything (paychecks, birthday, or holiday checks) for expensive items, emergencies, and retirement.

- **COMPOUND INTEREST:** It can work for or against you.

- **FIND BETTER DEALS:** Be a smart consumer.

- **UNDERSTAND WANTS, NEEDS, AND TRADE-OFFS:** Learn to delay gratification. Don't succumb to peer pressure.

- **HOW TO EARN CASH NOW:** Do you have a side gig or hobby that can be scaled to produce income? Find out if there's demand for your skills on service websites such as Taskrabbit, Thumbtack, or Angie's List.

- **DO NOT UNDER ANY CIRCUMSTANCES SHARE YOUR PIN, ACCOUNT, OR SOCIAL SECURITY NUMBER WITH ANYONE:** While it may seem like a good idea at the time, it will come back to haunt you.

There are websites online that can help. Mint.com offers a free budget app and tracker at https://www.mint.com. Also check out sites like Listen Money Matters, with helpful articles such as this one: "Money Tips for Teenagers" https://www.listenmoneymatters.com/money-tips-for-teenagers/.

PARACHUTE TIP

As with any college or university, deciding whether going to a community college will improve your employability totally depends on what you study. Learn more by reading "The Overlooked Value of Certificates and Associates Degrees: What Students Need to Know Before They Go to College" (https://cew.georgetown.edu/cew-reports/subba/) for more information on this topic. The Bureau of Labor Statistics predicts that today's teens will be in the workforce for fifty or sixty years. If you need a bachelor's degree for your ultimate career goal, you'll have plenty of time to acquire one. But do you need one right away? A university degree doesn't guarantee financial success after all, and people are financially successful with and without them.

> **"** After working for a few months, I have a better understanding of what skills I need to advance in my field. I have been able to identify what I can learn now in order to make my job better in the future. I love how inexpensive and flexible community college is for this purpose. **"**
>
> —Melanie Tolomeo, sales and marketing coordinator, Blue Planet Training

if you choose to go to work right out of high school, you can still go to college later. Think about how each step of a ladder takes you closer to the top—you can gain your education or training in steps too. Work a while to build your skills and bank account, identify a new job goal within your field, then go back to school. Repeat this cycle until you achieve your ultimate career goal. Generations of ambitious students have chosen this option as a way to achieve their educational goals without incurring large amounts of debt.

PARACHUTE TIP

Want to stand out? Get an internship in high school. Having internship experience gives you an advantage over dozens of college and technical program applicants. Internships can help you decide your college major and whether a certain job fits you.

REALITY CHECK

After twelve years of classes, the idea of more years of study may not thrill you. A technical certificate or license might take only a few months to finish, and can greatly boost your earning potential.

Can't face another day of school? Consider a "gap year." (You don't have to take a whole year—or you might take two.) This gap isn't a vacation paid for by your parents. This is focused time for work, career planning, volunteering, an internship, a few classes on subjects of strong interest, maybe some travel. This is the time to learn what you need to know to make better career plans. Ninety percent of teens who take a gap year return to school.

You can see that there are numerous factors to consider when deciding whether and when to go to college. The answer isn't an easy yes or no. It's important to remember that the choice you make today doesn't prevent you from making another choice later. Even if you feel you've made a wrong turn, you can choose another direction for your life and work later.

Author's note: Some high school students have reported that teachers and counselors treat them like losers if they admit they're not interested in a bachelor's degree right after graduation (even if they're good students just planning a gap year).

One reader of a previous edition of this book shared her story: "I'm one of the people who was looked down on for not going straight to college after high school. It seems like it's everywhere in today's culture. Shortly after I graduated, I got a full-time job at a supermarket. I felt like I lucked out because the job was close to home and I worked with an amazing team. I was told by a lot of supervisors that I was a good employee. I really enjoyed what I did and was looking to work for a couple years to save money to go to school later. I could definitely see myself going back to school at some point; just not right away."

This student's greatest need was to become completely self-supporting as quickly as she could after graduating from high school. She also had no burning career goals that needed a university education. She was thrilled to have found a good-paying job doing a variety of tasks, and to be seen as a productive team member. Given her circumstances, she made excellent choices. This is why *your* after-high-school plans should be created with your individual needs, goals, and resources in mind. No one path fits all. Your teachers' or counselors' prejudices ("Go to a liberal arts college versus a community college"; "Take out student loans instead of working first and saving"; "Any university degree is better than no degree"; "If you take a gap, you will probably not return to school") should be given zero weight and polite pushback.

Dual Enrollment

Dual enrollment is another way to make the most of your time in high school. Dual enrollment means you are enrolled in higher education while you are still in high school. While AP high school classes are similar to college courses, dual enrollment classes are truly college-level courses. It's a way to use your time in high school while checking out college classes and gaining credits. You won't be given any slack for being a teen, and will be graded against the same standards as adults in your class. You might want to take electives, general education requirements, or classes specific to your occupational choices through dual enrollment. Dual enrollment requirements vary by state and by school district, so research your local program. In the United States, there are nearly one million teens participating in dual enrollment. Get program information, including tips from a young participant, when you visit https://collegeinfogeek.com/dual-enrollment/.

Do I Even Need to Graduate from High School? Short Answer: Yes!

If by age sixteen you're bored beyond belief with high school, head over to your local community college and take the placement exams. Once you've passed them, consider enrolling. Many community colleges have programs that enable you to finish your high school diploma while taking college-level classes.

Can't pass the proficiency levels in math, science, or English? If you were to enroll in community college at this point, you would be put into remedial classes. The more remedial classes you take, the more likely you are to drop out: students who take just three remedial classes are 70 percent more likely to quit. Community college is your best and cheapest resource for education or training that leads to good jobs, so don't waste the opportunity. If you can't pass the exams at community college, redouble your efforts to learn in your high school classes. If you are behind in credits, in serious danger of not graduating with your class, and considering dropping out, talk with a counselor at a nearby community college where they have GED programs for teens.

> **❝** *A lot of so-called blue-collar trade jobs are now more highly paid than a lot of white-collar jobs. So, if we're talking about worthwhile jobs that are interesting, challenging, and well paid, then that sort of white-collar/blue-collar distinction is not a very good indication, any longer, of what goes on in the labor market.* **❞**
>
> —The Honorable Michael Cullen, New Zealand Minister
> of Higher Education and Finance, 2007

Postscript: Life after High School

Well-paying, interesting jobs require some amount of additional education or training beyond a high school diploma. That's the reality of today's job market. As we've discussed, you can continue higher education after you graduate from high school, or wait a couple of years. Not ready for college or advanced technical training now? After a few years of work, going back to school may be more appealing. Young adults returning to school after they've worked for several years often become great students. They have valuable work and life experience, and they are clear on what they want in life—so they go for it!

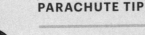

PARACHUTE TIP

Going to community college? Build a budget for three years. That's the average amount of time it takes young adults to complete a two-year degree. Going to a state college or university? Build your budget for five or six years. Only one out of three students finishes a bachelor's degree in four years.

High School: What's Happening Now

By Shawn Cowley, MBA, teacher and former soldier
www.linkedin.com/pub/shawn-cowley/0/55/38a

"You're joining the Army? Really? Why would you want to do that?" a high school classmate's mother condescendingly asked me back in 1984 in the spring of my senior year. I simply shrugged back then, but in hindsight, it was the wisest decision of my life.

First and foremost, I knew myself. I lacked the discipline and focus to steer away from the temptations of college at eighteen and avoid wasting thousands of dollars on an education without a clear objective. I recognized that I had no true career plan at that time. My high school wrestling coach, my father, the neighborhood parents—everyone greeted my decision with disappointment. My best friend said, "You would have been the ultimate frat boy!" "Exactly," I thought.

Only 50 percent of students who enter college actually graduate. A third of them drop out in their very first year. Yet still, in the school district that I work in, the over-whelming emphasis is placed on getting into college. Parents are doing a great job of taking students to visit college campuses, but they are not putting the same level of effort into exposing them to desired career fields.

Here's an example of why this is a problem. I've seen many students take an engaging and interesting psychology class in high school, then decide to pursue a career as a psychologist. Excited about the field, they go on to college and suddenly discover the rigor of the science classes required (side-by-side with premed students) and the necessity of a graduate degree, more school, more debt—all this with no clear path to becoming a practicing and employed psychologist. Discouraged, they quickly change majors or drop out.

The good news is that we are getting better. Many elective classes and extra-curricular activities are implementing career exploration into their curricula. A few examples: Future Business Leaders of America, Project Lead the Way (an engineering-based program), Junior ROTC (a character/citizenship program), and Distributive Education Clubs of America. More young men and women are taking advantage of the Boy Scouts of America's Explorers program and other internship-based programs to provide real-life experience in their career fields of interest. Apprenticeship2000.com is a fantastic program that puts students in an actual job while attending community college—an apprenticeship program styled after those in Europe. Our school district has brought back vocational-based learning in magnet schools.

Programs like these can provide you with pathways and mentorships from high school through advanced education, leading the way to jobs in desired and growing career fields. Exploring these opportunities may help you make the best decisions of *your* life.

What do *you* want to do after high school? Imagine you and your friends are brainstorming about the future. What ideas might you hear? What ideas would you contribute? Here are some possibilities:

- Travel—around the country or around the world.

- Take a gap year. No matter what you do or where you go, use your time to create plans for your first career path.

- Get a part-time or full-time job and continue your education (go to a two-year or four-year school, take online courses, get a technical certificate or license, or learn a skill or trade).

- Get a part-time job and do volunteer work to learn more skills and to make contacts that will help you in your job search.

- Get any job in your favorite field or industry to learn more about it.

- Figure out a job that could be in demand anywhere in the world. Get qualified. Go.

- Check out a new city or state (or even country!) to live in.

- Look into studying or living abroad.

- Volunteer for an international or domestic program helping others through your house of worship or other community organization.

- Begin a registered federal apprenticeship. There are over 1,000 federal apprenticeships in dozens of industries. (All building trade apprenticeships are administered by the federal Department of Labor.)

- Create your own apprenticeship.

- Use and improve your problem-solving skills by working on one of the seventeen United Nations Sustainable Development Goals (https://sustainabledevelopment.un.org/?menu=1300)

- Get a fun job, even if it's not what you want for a career.

- Join the Peace Corps, State Civilian Conservation Corps, Job Corps, or AmeriCorps. Information about these organizations is available online.

- Join the military.

Getting ideas? Add them to the list. What are your top three choices? Whatever you choose to do, do it with your whole heart. Live your life to the fullest. Your twenties are an important time to establish a good foundation for your career. They should also be fun.

CHAPTER 6

What Do I Do Next? Make the Most of the Best and Least Expensive Higher Education

> **66** *Where you go after high school—whether you go to college and which college you go to—is much less important than what you study.* **99**
>
> —Rich Feller, PhD, professor and author of
> *Knowledge Nomads and the Nervously Employed*

For the life you want as a twenty-something, do you need an education or to earn a living? With planning you can get both. Without planning, it's easy to get neither. If you want a broad education with access to lots of different classes while majoring in a specific subject for your bachelor's degree, that's a university education. If you want to earn a living in specific skill or trade, you don't need a university degree. Getting a bachelor's degree at a university is a big investment of time and money. There's a lot to consider when it comes to ensuring you get what you want from your time at university, and this chapter will cover getting a bachelor's degree in detail. After graduating from high school or getting a GED, obtaining certificates online or going to a trade school are two additional ways to qualify for employment.

What is a trade school? Simply put, it's a school where you can learn a trade. They are also known as vocational, career, or technical schools. Some trade schools focus on teaching the skills for only one trade. Others offer multiple trade-learning opportunities. For example, community colleges teach multiple trade and technical skills, and also offer academic courses that allow you to transfer to a bachelor's program at a college or university. Community colleges are supported by both tuition fees and your state's department of education. Tuition at a public community college is usually less than a private for-profit trade school. Before you enroll at a private trade school, find out if a community college offers the same training. Even if you need to move to a different part of your state to access community college training, it still may be cheaper and more preferred by employers than a for-profit school.

Private for-profit trade schools have gotten a reputation for being predatory, pressuring low-income students and veterans to borrow money, and saddling their students with tens of thousands of dollars of debt without providing the necessary training for students to become employable. A glossy brochure or slick website doesn't guarantee the school will help you get a job. Faculty at private for-profit schools don't always have appropriate credentials, and may not teach at a level that will help students pass state certification tests. Online schools are cheaper to run than brick and mortar schools, but trade and technical skills require real-time practice. If the trade you want to learn needs hands-on training, find out how to get this critical part of your education before you enroll in an online program.

True story: I interviewed a young woman who was $10,000 in debt after enrolling at a private for-profit school to be a stewardess. She hadn't done enough research to know that each airline in the United States trains its own flight attendants. When asked what made her pick this school, she said, "Well, they had a really great website and were located at a big airport." Thorough research can save you time, money, embarrassment, and heartache.

PARACHUTE TIP

If you want to learn a trade, check with employers for whom you hope to work. From what schools do they usually hire employees?

While there are reputable private for-profit trade schools, there are way too many that aren't. If you are considering a trade or technical school, use this checklist:

1. Is the school accredited?

2. If so, is the program accredited by a recognized accreditation agency? For-profits may have their own accreditation agencies, which means the accreditation is worthless.

3. What percentage of its students complete the program?

4. What percentage of students who graduate pass the licensing exam for that profession?

5. What percentage of the faculty is licensed in the field?

6. Does the school have a review program for those who graduate but don't pass the exam?

7. Can the school connect you with program graduates?

More information about trade and technical school options can be found at:

- https://getschooled.com/article/4600-alternative-to-college-badge-what-is-a-trade-school/

- https://www.ntinow.edu/blog/difference-trade-school-college/

- https://thebestschools.org/degrees/trade-schools/

REALITY CHECK

Avoid attending private, for-profit certificate granting institutions. Six years after graduation, graduates with certificates from for-profit higher education schools were earning less than a high school graduate. Not a good ROI. This and other fascinating information come from an exhaustive Third Way report done in 2019 https://www.thirdway.org/report/the-state-of-american-higher-education-outcomes-in-2019.

If you go to the website, look at the State of Higher Ed spreadsheet, which has data on over 4,000 institutions. This data includes the percentages of students who graduate, earn more than a high school graduate, and have been able to pay down their student loans. This study only includes students who took out federal student loans. If that's going to be you, check out the institutions you are considering attending. If institutions you want to attend aren't on this list, call or email directly to get this information. As a consumer, you have the right to know. If you intend to go to an institution with a low success rate, you'd better have a serious plan to make sure you don't drop out, overborrow, or become underemployed.

And then there's Google. Like other tech firms, Google noticed a huge supply mismatch that left too many unfilled positions. In early 2021, they launched new certification programs in which college degrees are not necessary. The certification programs are designed to eliminate skills gaps and get people qualified for well-paying, high-growth jobs in tech.

The plan includes:

- Continuous development of new Google Career Certificates through Coursera. Currently offered are certificates in Project Management, Data Analytics, User Experience (UX) Design, and an Associate Android Developer Certification course

- Over 100,000 need-based scholarships in the United States

- Partnerships with over 130 employers working with Google to hire certificate program graduates

- A new Google Search feature that makes it easier for people to find jobs for their education level, with or without a degree or experience

Most course work costs less than $300 and can be completed in six months; courses completed in three months cost half. The course work is rigorous (each certificate has about 100 assessments), but passing assessments guarantees a person has the skills to do a certain job.

By creating a pipeline for nontraditional talent and decreasing traditional barriers, Google hopes to help accelerate economic recovery and provide millions the opportunity to find a job, grow their careers, and start or expand a business. Learn about Google's certification programs at https://grow.google/certificates.

Fifty-five percent of tech executives hire workers without college degrees. This number is likely to grow. Like Coursera, Udemy and Udacity also partner with tech companies to offer online certification in IT support, cloud computing, and data analysis. While remote work will remain popular, it doesn't mean you don't have to interact with coworkers. In addition to appropriate certifications, the strongest candidates will be able to work in teams, collaborate well, and communicate effectively.

❝ *The best businesses will hire on the basis of a worker's skill, not academic credentials. Given the rising cost of college and the worsening economic conditions because of COVID-19, paying for college imposes a significant financial burden on most families. As more workers opt for alternative forms of training, the future of talent management will crucially rely on identifying talented workers among the more than 50 percent of the US workforce who don't have a college degree.* **❞**

—Peter Blair, Harvard assistant professor

Going to college? Great! If you have completed the Discovery Exercises in Part One, you a have a big advantage over the 75 percent of students who begin college not knowing what they want to study. If you don't know what you want to study, how do you know you need a bachelor's degree? If you have completed your Parachute and used it to identify jobs you want, you already know what you need to study. Knowing your intended major or what courses to take saves you money and time. Eighty percent of university students change majors at least once. The average university student changes majors three times. Each major change costs approximately $10,000, or 10 percent of the total cost of your bachelor's degree. That means the average university student unnecessarily adds at least $30,000 to the total cost of their education. Forty percent of the students who start any form of higher education drop out. Many who quit say they had no idea why they were in college, and were not fully committed to completing their education. Knowing that your career needs a bachelor's degree gives you a strong motivation to finish.

In the 1960s, '70s, and into the '80s, young adults went to university to discover what they wanted to do. Most found good jobs after graduation simply because they had a university degree. You do not live in that world. In your world, a college degree doesn't guarantee either employment or high pay. Currently, less than half of recent grads with bachelor's degrees have found work that requires their level of education. Nearly thirteen of every 100 university grads are making $25,000 or less. The tricky bit is that low-paying jobs are being created faster than high-paying jobs. On average, the lower earning half of university grads earn only $1,900 more per year than the average high school graduate. At the moment, the unemployment rate of recent university graduates is higher than the unemployment rate of all US workers. This is not intended to discourage you from going to university if you need a bachelor's degree for the work you want to do. It is meant to underscore that you must make sure getting a bachelor's degree will pay off for you. To make that happen, you must juggle academics and career development. Along with your studies, you need to learn about the labor market where you want to live, work on your career goals, and expand your contacts while in school. Don't treat your college education like a very expensive lottery ticket: tens of thousands of dollars spent for the chance at a good job. Through research, planning, and action you can make it a sure thing.

Higher Education Is an Investment in Yourself

"Investment" is defined as putting money into something now, in anticipation of profit or material result in the future. Higher education can be a classic investment; money invested now will make more money later. Poorly planned, higher education can also be an epic financial failure. The top risks to your education investment are:

1. Dropping out with debt and no degree. You have increased your financial liability without improving your employability. In 2018, the unemployment rate of high school dropouts was 13.7 percent, and the unemployment rate of college dropouts was 18.6 percent—more than five points higher.

2. Overborrowing and using all your financial resources to get your first degree.

3. Not taking advantage of opportunities to improve your employability while in college.

Getting the Most Out of College

Your college years can be fun and very rewarding in many ways, but they also require a new sense of responsibility for your personal life and future financial health. It's up to you to make your university education pay off. The suggestions in the checklist below are from current and former college students. Setting up time to go through them will help you get the most out of the effort and money you are investing in yourself through higher education. Whether you are still in high school, a recent graduate starting university, or going into college as an older young adult, this list helps you get the best return on your education investment.

Set up time to complete them. Which ones can you do before you start school? During your first semester? As a sophomore, junior, or senior? During semester breaks or summers?

The number one tip from previous students: get to know your professors, and let them get to know you. Go to their office hours—times they've set aside for students to stop by their office, ask questions, and discuss assignments—in the first two weeks. Introduce yourself before asking for a favor or raising an issue that needs their attention. Reading articles or research they've written will give you something to chat about.

- Make a financial plan. Get help creating a budget for yourself. Know how much you can spend on food, necessities, and entertainment each day, week, and month.

- Eat a good breakfast.

- Learn how to prioritize tasks and manage your time well. For the rest of your life, you'll have competing priorities, so knowing how to perform well while juggling multiple tasks is a skill you'll need. Make daily goals. Write the top three things you need to get done each day on a large sticky note and post it someplace visible.

- As a freshman, get engaged in activities on campus that interest you. Participate in an academic area, leadership, social issue, politics, sport, occupational interest, or hobby. Students who have met their professors and are involved with interest groups are less likely to drop out. Engaging with adult faculty and staff pays off with letters of recommendation, building a network, and uncovering opportunities.

- Take classes outside your comfort zone. These expand your worldview and your creativity.

- Find the best professors you can. Don't ignore the 8:00 a.m. class taught by a terrific professor. Whether taking classes in your major or an elective, you get more bang for your education buck with good teachers. Most colleges have websites with student evaluations of professors, and most students are willing to share feedback about professors they have had.

- Take classes that use real-world situations to teach about life and work. Consider leadership development, foreign language, business communications, or entrepreneurship courses.

- Run for office. Student government is a way to get to know faculty, staff, and other students. You will be exposed to a broad range of issues and concerns.

- Don't be intimidated by small seminar classes. You can learn exponentially more than in huge, anonymous, lecture-hall survey classes.

- Find your college's learning resource center. What resources do they have to help you learn effective study skills? Unless you got a perfect SAT (2400) or ACT (36) score, you'll probably need to amp up your study skills from high school level.

- Learn to think critically, which includes recognizing and filtering out unnecessary information.

- Exercise as regularly as possible. Your mind and body will thank you.

- Acquire social skills and build friendships. The ability to do both will enrich your personal and professional lives.

- Join clubs and organizations that let you explore career interests. Find students with similar career interests so you can explore together, and have much more fun.

- Get to know your alumni network sooner than later. Don't wait until graduation. Find out when your department will hold its next alumni event, then when you go, practice your social skills while building contacts. Alums can answer field-related questions and give you tips on good professors, internships, summer jobs, or permanent ones.

- Plan for multiple internships or a part-time position to immerse you in the realities of the jobs you think you want.

- At least once a term, pick a class that absolutely fascinates you. Let your interest lead you toward learning beyond what is needed for a good grade. Future employers want you to know how to analyze, synthesize, evaluate, theorize, and connect seemingly unrelated information.

- Have a Plan B. Life can be extremely unpredictable. Should something happen to prevent you from continuing your education, you'll already have another path in mind.

PARACHUTE TIP

The best get-the-most-out-of-college book is Suzette Tyler's *Been There, Should Have Done That: 995 Tips for Making the Most of College*. Make your parents read it with you. If they went to college, they may groan over all the opportunities they didn't know about and missed!

Financial Realities of College and Academic Degrees

The financial realities of college affect your life not only while you're in college, but for years afterward if you borrowed money through student loans or credit cards. If your parents are paying for part or all of your education, doing so impacts their lives and possibly their ability to retire.

Your high school teachers may tell you that you must get a bachelor's degree "no matter what it costs." Some folks may tell you that all student loan debt is good debt.

Don't listen. These well-meaning people won't be the ones paying off *your* student loans. Have you ever paid off $500 of debt? Depending on your starting salary after graduation, having five to ten thousand dollars of debt can make life hard. Someone who advises you to go into debt for a bachelor's degree when you know neither how much you might need to borrow, nor if your starting salary will cover your loan repayment, is not your friend. It's unlikely that the federal government will wipe out all student loan debt. Currently, you aren't eligible for federal student loan forgiveness until you've worked for ten years, and only 2 percent of those who applied have been granted loan forgiveness. This is why it's important to carefully research the cost of the education you need, and buy only as much education as you can afford.

Here are two good articles about the intricacies of student loan forgiveness: "What You Should Know about Public Service Loan Forgiveness (PSLF)" at https://www.debt.com/student-loan-debt/forgiveness-program/pslf/ and a summary of the Public Service Loan Forgiveness issues and requirements at https://www.whitecoatinvestor.com/public-service-loan-forgiveness/.

> **66** *A designer degree doesn't matter nearly as much in the long run as the things a student does while getting that piece of paper—especially the activities and jobs between classes and during the summer. Those are the things that will truly contribute to a depth of self-discovery, transforming college students into adults with not only education but confidence, job skills, and a global perspective too.* **99**
>
> —Holly Robinson, author and blogger

Almost all private student loans are bad debt. Private variable interest loans have no reasonable cap on the amount of interest or fees you can be charged. They are not regulated by the government and don't qualify for federal repayment programs. Unless there is no alternative and you need to borrow only a small amount, avoid private student loans.

Research starting salaries for the jobs you want. Salaries for experienced workers are important for career decision making but a big caution: it's your starting salary that determines how much you can afford to borrow for your degree or training. Once you know the likely starting salaries for jobs that interest you, take that number, divide it by three, and multiply it by two. The resulting number is the **TOTAL** amount you can afford to borrow.

It's a mistake to assume that all academic degrees translate into increased earnings when you join the workforce—they don't. According to US News (2019), petroleum engineering, which is the highest paid college major, has a median starting salary that's $61,000 more than the two lowest paid majors—child development and psychology. The media and universities make much of the average starting salary of $50,000 for bachelor's degrees in 2020. That's a decent starting wage, but it's skewed upward by the starting salaries of about a dozen high-paying majors. You're not going to make that amount unless you study for and get a job that pays a starting salary of $50,000.

Make no assumptions about the pay of the jobs you want. Salary information sites such as Salary.com, Glassdoor, and PayScale can be helpful. This salary report from the National Association of Colleges and Employers (2019) covers many majors: https://www.utdallas.edu/career/docs/about/NACESalary2019.pdf). As salaries vary widely throughout the country, check with employers (often the human resource department) in the city where you want to live. When doing starting salary research, remember that average and median are not equivalent.

Earning Power and Debt

Let's say that you and your college roommate have spent the same amount of $135,000 to earn bachelor of science degrees. Completing your degrees took each of you five years at a total cost of $27,000 per year (for tuition and fees, room and board; books, supplies, transportation, and personal expenditures). You each borrow $37,000 in student loans. The average monthly repayment for this amount of debt is $400. Your roommate graduates with a degree in computer science. She accepts a full-time job with a starting salary of $67,500. Your degree is in exercise physiology. Starting salaries average $38,500 where you want to live. The best job offer you've gotten so far is for twenty-six hours a week at $20.05 an hour. (This example uses 2019 averages.)

PARACHUTE TIP

Before thinking about loans, fill out a FAFSA (Free Application Form for Federal Student Aid) form at http://studentaid.ed.gov/fafsa. It's your portal to federal loans. If you are eligible for any federal grants, aid, or work-study funds, this form helps you apply for them. High school students are encouraged to start looking at them in their junior year. The FAFSA form is complicated; don't wait until two days before the deadline to fill it out.

How does your financial situation compare with that of your roommate? Even if you get full-time work, it's going to take you years longer to pay off your student loan debt than it will for your roommate. That $37,000 can double in less than ten years through interest and charges for late or missed payments. How much you borrow for your degree and your salary after graduation will affect where you live (50 percent of recent college grads move back home), if you can afford a car, how quickly or slowly you become debt free, and what you can afford to do in your free time. Remember that in addition to paying off your student loan debt, you need to start saving for both retirement and emergencies. Young adults really need to begin saving for their retirement by age twenty-five, contributing at least $1,500 a year.

Another statistic you'll hear tossed about is that on average, bachelor's degree holders earn a million dollars more throughout their work lives than those with a high school diploma only. (Conveniently overlooked in this hyperbolic dichotomy are lifetime earning averages for those with technical or associate degrees.) The chemical engineer who graduated with $100,000 of debt and had a forty-year career earning an average of $75,000 a year may achieve that milestone. The person who spent $140,000 for their teaching degree—a field in which starting salaries average $38,620—and earned an average of $59,000 over their forty-year career will not. Future earning power is all about what you study, and how much you owe.

Living on Top Ramen noodles is something many college students do. By your mid-twenties, knowing friends can afford to party at the latest hip brewpub while you can barely afford a frozen dinner is very disheartening (not to mention of dubious nutritional value). For young adults whose dream jobs pay less than $40,000 a year and who would need to borrow more than $26,000 to gain their desired degree, education-work ladders are an excellent option. A ladder allows you to step up and reach higher; education-work ladders do the same. Get enough qualifications to make a first (entry-level) step in your chosen field, work a bit, save money, go back to school, then step up to the next rung in your field. Education-work ladders can get you the qualifications you need for jobs you want, without your becoming an indentured servant to student loans. If you are a valued employee in a competitive field, some employers will help pay for further education and training.

Overestimating the cost of higher education is as bad as underestimating the value of an opportunity you could have afforded, but turned down. You'll want to learn the costs for each school you are considering, and the average student loan interest rate. Then you can use one of many online student loan calculators to determine what you will actually pay over the life of the loan, and what your monthly payment will be. The resulting sticker price is your tuition. The cost can be reduced through scholarships, work-study, and grants. Those who need help with this net price seek student loans. Remember that tuition and fees are part, but not the total cost, of a year of education. Most schools can give you an estimate of average total cost. If you need to work more than half-time, budget three years for community college and six for a bachelor's degree. In 2020, the average tuition and fees were:

- $4,811 community college for in-state students; and $8,584, out-of-state students

- $10,116 public university, in-state

- $22,577 public university, out-of-state

- $36,801 private university

- $50,000+ private, elite university

> 66 *Don't take on too much debt. Most students would be smart to limit their total borrowing to no more than two-thirds of the annual salary they expect to make in their first year after college. If you're at or near that limit and haven't finished your schooling, consider transferring to a cheaper college or taking a year off to work and pay down your loans.* 99
>
> —Liz Pulliam Weston, MSN Money Central

Higher education debt is a major issue for college students, their parents, and their grandparents. Elder US citizens are having social security checks garnished to pay off old student loans! About a third of college graduates leave school in serious financial difficulty. According to college officials, more students drop out of college due to debt than due to bad grades. College students who don't take the time to for careful financial planning, making career connections, selecting job targets, and having internships before graduation are more likely to work minimum-wage jobs unrelated to their studies, or to be unemployed. There is no loan repayment deferment just because you can't find a job.

With the current financial realities of college in mind, how can you make the most out of your college years, particularly in terms of finding work you'll love? Continue to increase your awareness of jobs in your favorite fields or industries. Apply for internships. Hone your job-search skills. The difference from high school is that you'll do these things with more depth, enthusiasm, and focus, since you'll be much closer to the day when you'll need to go out and use your skills to land a good job.

Licensing

In addition to a degree, do the best jobs in your field require a license? If they do, you'll need to budget time to study for them, and money to pay for the tests and to support you while you study. Employers love licenses. Why? For most licenses, you need a test score of 70 percent or higher to pass. To an employer, your ability to pass a licensing exam means you have enough knowledge or skills to function on the job. Grades give no such guarantee.

> 66 *The way we have funded higher education in this country has had the unintended consequence of indenturing an entire generation of students who now comprise the "educated poor."* 99
>
> —Robert Applebaum, lawyer and founder of forgivestudentloandebt.com

> **66** People need to approach college like they approach purchasing a car. Different people can afford different models. Don't be deterred from going to college, but students need to be smart shoppers. **99**
>
> —Anya Kamenetz, journalist and author of *Generation Debt and DIY U*

PARACHUTE TIP

Personal savings plans run from the extremely simple ($52 saved at $1 a week; $1040 saved at $20 per week) to the extremely complex, using percentages of income. Try the "52-Week Money Challenge": save $1 week one, $2 week two, and so on. By the end of the year you'll have saved $1,387!

Cultivate Qualities, Develop Skills

As you select your classes, major, and extracurricular activities, keep in mind what employers look for in college graduate new hires. Data literacy, critical thinking, tech savvy, adaptability and flexibility, and creativity were the top five skills employers wanted in 2021. Those are followed by emotional intelligence, cultural intelligence, understanding diversity, leadership skills, judgment and complex decision-making, and collaboration. The skills employers want are constantly changing. Do an internet search to keep yourself up to date on what skills employers favor. Plan your courses, extracurricular activities, internships, or volunteer work so that you are proficient in the qualities and skills employers want. In hiring interviews, ask your interviewer what skills they most want in new employees. Anyone hoping to get hired in the field or job of their dreams should be able to provide examples and demonstrate these skills in hiring interviews.

In college and on the job, success means showing up 99 percent of the time. One quality employers demand is a strong work ethic. This means that you're not only present but willing to work hard; you're dependable, responsible, and punctual; you take your work seriously; and you do that work as well as you possibly can. Having a strong work ethic can get you hired; lacking one can get you fired.

Information interviews and job shadowing let you observe work ethics in operation at each place of business. Behavior encouraged by one employer may not be expected—or tolerated—by another. You need to find a good fit between your own work ethic and that of your employer. When you have a job interview, *you* are actually interviewing the *employer* as much as the employer is interviewing you.

> **Shut off your cell phones, cover your body, turn off the video poker, unplug your iPod, stop text messaging your friends, and get to work.**
>
> —Young Silicon Valley executive to recent college grads

Make Contacts

In addition to developing the qualities and skills that employers want most, it's important to use your college years to gain work experience and develop relationships with your professors and supervisors. Information interviews, job shadowing, internships, part-time jobs, and summer jobs are good ways to expand the range of people you know. Keep a list of people you meet, their contact information, and how you met them. LinkedIn.com has terrific suggestions for connecting with people for career advice and information.

Information Interviews and Job Shadowing in College

Continue doing information interviews as you did in high school, only more often and in greater depth. Ask to meet with people for twenty to thirty minutes. Request more detail about the day-to-day realities of their jobs and the direction they see their field taking—including what opportunities or obstacles that might present for you. Ask about how climate change, AI, robotics, and other technical innovations will impact their work.

Chapter 5 offered some basic information about job shadowing. You can use the same technique in college to learn more about specific jobs. Now that you have additional life, academic, and work experience, perhaps you're more curious about certain jobs, and will be more comfortable asking questions. Better questions get better information.

Can your college career center help find people (perhaps alumni) for you to job shadow or interview? Faculty members in your major, college roommates, friends, even their parents may also provide important contacts. Get in touch with your college's office of alumni relations. Good schools have databases about their grads that include employment information. Read one or two professional journals regularly. Get in touch with the authors of articles that interest you. (If you find you have no interest in reading a professional journal, how can you contemplate working in that field?)

Don't forget those people you job shadowed or did information interviews with when you were in high school. If your interests still lie in the same area, consider contacting them again for suggestions and opportunities.

Information interviews are so critical to getting high-quality information about the work you want to do. But they can be hard to set up, especially the first few. People in high visibility jobs can get burned out being frequently asked for their time. People working in smaller companies may be easier to approach. Remember, it usually takes asking a couple of people, "Do you know someone who . . . ?" to get linked with a connection.

College Internships

College internships are designed to introduce you to a particular field or job, and to give you practical work experience. Generally, they last longer than high school internships. Employers prefer to hire college students who have done multiple internships. They value internship experience higher than grades, the college you attended, and even your professional recommendations. Ninety-one percent of employers don't care where you went to school. They want you to be able to do what they need you to do.

Check with the career center at your college for information on internships. Many companies and businesses offer internships to college students. Some are paid and some are not; some take place during the summer, others during the school year. Some company internships are only open to students from a certain college. Others are open nationally and internationally. Professional associations are a good source for internship leads as well. Want to be a vintner? The vintners' association in the region where you want to live may know of internship opportunities.

Internships with major companies are very competitive. Why? In addition to gaining valuable skills and well-known professional contacts, Fortune 500 internships pay between $5,000 and $9,000 per month. If you want this kind of internship experience, during your sophomore year start taking the classes and getting the experience companies want prospective interns to have. If you're unable to find an internship that fits your particular needs, try contacting several companies that you'd like to work for. Can you set up an internship directly with one of them? You can find instructions online for setting up this kind of independent internship.

The quality of internships varies wildly; some students report being active members of a team, while others say they just warmed a chair. Your professors may know of students who have done internships that interest you—request a connection so you can interview them. Avoid internships that are a waste of time. Make sure you do your part: show up on time, professionally dressed and open to new assignments. Take on long-term projects, such as data entry, to keep yourself busy even when you don't have a particular assignment. If your experience is a good one, after you graduate you may be offered a full-time position at the business where you interned. Sixty-six percent of students who had paid internships got job offers. Only 44 percent of unpaid interns were offered full-time jobs. Even if you don't get a job offer, internships build new skills, greater confidence, and strengthen your resume. If you impress the people you worked with, they may offer to write professional references for you, or connect you with potential employers.

PARACHUTE TIP

When you finish a class, an internship, a volunteer project, or a job where you did particularly good work or were complimented for your contributions, ask for a letter of recommendation before you leave. Even if your supervisor or professor likes and remembers you, he or she may have trouble remembering the details of your work after a few months. Get it in writing!

Internships: More to the Experience Than a Job Offer

By Mark Babbitt, CEO of YouTern
www.linkedin.com/in/marksbabbitt
mark@youtern.com

The controversy over paid versus unpaid internships is not the hot topic it was just a few short years ago. As a result, more college students and recent graduates are completing several internships during or just after their college years than ever before. Their goal: shortly after graduation, secure that elusive first "real" job.

However, surveys show us that interns are offered a job from their current or last employer about 50 percent of the time. Why are so many young careerists committed to completing internships? Here are five really good reasons . . .

A Degree Is Not Enough

Those students who still believe a high GPA and a degree are enough to land them a job after graduation are living in denial. Even worse, many seem to still be living the "Big Lie"—one told by educators, academics, and parents for decades: a college degree makes each one of us employable.

This is simply not true and hasn't been since about 1994. With entry-level jobs almost extinct, new hires are expected to contribute from day one. Today's employers look for direct relevant experience—the kind that enables new team members to hit the ground running. They also look for emotional intelligence, or EQ (how you work as an individual within the work environment), and workplace intelligence, or WQ (how well you work within an existing team and company culture).

And what's the best way to gain EQ and WQ? Internships.

One Can Never Have Enough Mentors

There is another common factor among successful students and recent grads: they deliberately seek out multiple mentors within their chosen industry while completing an internship.

Career mentors are a special combination of adviser, sheriff, confidant, listener, and accountability partner. They keep you focused. Through their experience, they shorten learning curves. The good ones encourage the expansion of your thought processes as you meet new challenges. They open minds—and hearts.

Perhaps most important, a good mentor helps the student navigate the wide chasm between academic life and the real world.

Making Sure Your Career Choice Is Right for You

Many college students agonize over which college major to pursue. They work hard to earn a degree that is both attractive to them and the right employer. Yet, few students exert the level of effort required before graduation to ensure that degree is the right one for them. This is especially true for "first-gen" students—those who are the first in their family to pursue a college education.

Nearly every day, we hear stories of accounting majors who spent four to six years in school then once they enter the field, they truly dislike accounting. Or law school graduates who despise being attorneys. Or veterinary technicians who discover their jobs are not always about helping animals, but more about cleaning up the mess when something goes wrong.

When chosen well, internships validate our career choices by offering real life experiences that show what the job really is versus some romanticized notion of what it should be. And when we wish to use an educational do-over, internships help us correct our career paths and avoid costly professional mistakes.

Is Graduate School the Right Choice?

Perhaps a more relevant question given the massive student load debt most graduates face: within your chosen career field, is graduate school even necessary?

Through 2012, 42 percent of recent grads felt a master's degree would make them more employable. According to a survey of 2019 graduates, that number has dropped to just 15 percent.

Why? Today's graduates are finding out that few really need graduate school. They realize the debt accrued, combined with the loss of earnings during five or more years of higher education may not be a wise investment. They find their time is better spent developing mentor relationships, mastering in-demand soft skills, and building a strong personal network.

In other words, many find they compete well in the job market not by staying in school—but through the experiential education found with internships. And if they do need a master's degree to get ahead? Well, those campuses will still be there when they decide to go back.

The Mastery of In-Demand Soft Skills

Perhaps the most important reason to pursue internships while in college, or immediately after graduation, is to gain soft skills. For the past decade, employers have reported the lack of workplace readiness as the number one issue for recent graduates; they are unaware of what it takes to succeed in the world of work. Specifically, employers state that while grads are technically savvy enough, they lack the soft skills necessary to hit the ground running.

Today's best employers don't just look at a candidate's educational background and work experience. They seek out those potential employees who have demonstrated a mastery of the soft skills most important to their company and to specific work teams. Examples of soft skills include communication, analytical thinking, problem solving, relationship building, collaboration, and leadership skills.

In other words, employers look for skills that can't be learned in books. Even in the most dynamic educational setting, soft skills can't be picked up in a classroom. These practical, been-there-done-that skills can only be learned by doing, experiencing, and sometimes by failing.

Internships don't guarantee a job offer. They do, however, create a foundation on which to build a successful early career. Making it your goal to complete at least one high-impact internship for each year of college will move you right to the top of the job-search competition!

PARACHUTE TIP

Go for internships in your teens. Montana-born Brad Bird, director of *The Incredibles*, was a Disney apprentice at fifteen years old. Millennial freelance writer Anya Kamenetz was fifteen when she had her first newspaper internship. After high school, Anya continued to find internships and get jobs at magazines to sharpen her skills, and eventually became well-paid and successful—not an easy achievement in the world of freelance writing. Read about Anya online to learn the steps she took. www.anyakamenetz.net

You as a Business

Young adults are referred to as "start-up adults." It's an interesting and helpful metaphor, as it alludes that a person is like the first phase of business just starting up. No business would spend $80,000 to $150,000+ (the cost of a bachelor's degree) on a new piece of equipment or a service without knowing how it would benefit them. Smart college-goers won't either. As with a business, you need a plan. The goal of your business plan is to leave college without crushing debt, with a job you'll like, in a career that makes use of your expensive college education.

REALITY CHECK

Start building your LinkedIn profile in high school or early in college. It's where nearly all would-be employers will go to find out about you. LinkedIn is your go-to site to find internships, alumni, top employers, and others to talk to about the work you want to do. Until you and your academic or career adviser are satisfied with your profile, watch a LinkedIn tutorial once a week. Start at https://university.linkedin.com/linkedin-for-students

If you did no career planning before starting college, follow this timeline to catch up.

Summer of freshman year (but winter or spring break is ideal): Start your Parachute and complete enough information interviews to learn about three fields or industries that interest you. What jobs or job clusters seem to overlap your Parachute? What internships are available through your university? Which ones will help you check out your job interests? Keep a list of names and contact information of all the people you meet who work in your chosen field. Reading a few professional journals may help you decide between fields.

Sophomore year: Use breaks to investigate those careers. You want to know which field or industry appeals to you most so that you can declare a major by the start of your junior year. Two out of every ten university sophomores drop out before their junior year because they don't know what major they want to pursue. Research shows that students who aren't sure what they want to do with their major, or who change majors more than once, are more likely to get jobs that don't use their college degree. Before winter break, identify internships you want. What are the application deadlines? If you want to study abroad, this is the year to apply.

Summer of sophomore year: Get an entry-level job or internship in the industry that interests you most, or set up a series of volunteer internships in several fields. Update your contact list. What have you learned that will help you successfully transition from school to work? What do you still need to learn? Update your plan for success.

Junior year: Identify the top ten employers for whom you'd like to work. Apply for international internships. Employers want graduates who are global citizens. Find professional conferences or local professional association meetings to attend.

Summer of junior year: Secure an internship or job in your field. Identify the top five or ten employers for whom you want to work. Find contacts at those organizations. Set up information interviews with those contacts. Update your contact list and your plan for success.

Senior year: Organize your classes so that you can complete another internship before you graduate. Keep learning about potential employers, and add another five to ten to your list. Get in touch with all of your contacts to let them know you are actively looking for work. Ask if they have contacts with your preferred employers, or have heard of any job openings. If no openings come up, reach out and introduce yourself to hiring managers to request a meeting. Schedule meetings by video chat if you can't afford the time or money to travel to these employers. This is a sales meeting; you are selling yourself as a qualified potential employee. Even if there are no jobs currently open, you could get referrals for some in the future. Seniors who have a job by the time they graduate report that it took six to nine months of active job searching to secure it.

66 *Your choices in college matter more than your choices of college.* **99**

—Peter D. Feaver, Sue Wasiolek, and Anne Crossman, authors of *Getting the Best Out of College*

Decisions, Decisions

Before making a final decision on whether to go to college or which colleges are the best match for you, here are some of the issues you'll need to consider, research, and evaluate: liberal arts or career-track major; private or public university; community college or university; double major or major and minor; living at home or on campus; taking a gap or going to university right after high school.

Before you commit to a school, check out the quality of career centers, resources to overcome learning disabilities, diversity and inclusivity, campus safety, residential-life programs, and access to counselors that help with long- or short-term personal issues.

The College Experience

Though our focus in this book is on helping you find work you'll love, life is more than just work. In addition to providing you with academic grounding, the college experience also challenges you to discover your true values. You may get involved in sports, volunteer work, clubs, or other activities that you'll continue for decades.

Challenges and responsibilities that you didn't have to worry about while you were in high school and living at home, but will encounter in college will help you grow and mature. Problems may include learning to work out differences with roommates, facing new financial realities, balancing study time with social time and work obligations, and maintaining an apartment (cleaning, grocery shopping, laundry, and cooking). If you ignore the challenges of college life and just party for four or five years, you'll waste not only a lot of money, but also your opportunity to prepare for finding satisfying work after college. College is not the end of your career development. It's one way to qualify for work you'll love.

No time in life is quite like your college years. It's nerve wracking, but it's also very special. While learning and having fun, you can continue building a strong foundation for your future.

PARACHUTE TIP

Having trouble with study skills or understanding academic content? Ask for help! Find your college learning resource center. Utilize department assistants or tutors if you need them. If you're having difficulty with a particular class, talk with the professor or teaching assistant. Don't wait—do this as soon as you feel like you are floundering. Your initiative in getting help indicates a strong work ethic and a drive toward success.

REALITY CHECK

Seventy percent of the young adults who enter college intending to go on to graduate school never do. Why is that a problem? Many of them chose majors (such as biology, animal science, psychology, for example) that don't have good salaries or prospects in the job market without that graduate degree. Students who realize by their sophomore year that grad school is unlikely would be wise to switch to a major with better salary and stronger employment opportunities.

CHAPTER 7

Goal Setting: Turn Wishes into Reality and Move Forward

---

66 *A goal is a dream with a deadline.* **99**

—Napoleon Hill, author of the classic book *Think and Grow Rich,* 1937

As you've been reading the previous chapters, completing the exercises, and answering questions, you've been gathering information on your interests, skills, and potential dream jobs. This research has helped you discover your likes, dislikes, and hopes. You've read about using high school and college experiences to enhance your awareness of the work world and job readiness. Has this exploration given you ideas about how your interests shape your potential work and your future? Goal setting is a tool that will help you do both.

A goal is something you want to achieve—such as learning to drive a car, getting a high school or college diploma, or representing your school in a competition. A goal can be a desire to experience something—such as traveling, going whitewater rafting, or meeting someone you've long admired. Your goals may be personal: improving social skills, reading a particular book, or learning to get along with your little sister. Others may be academic: being admitted into college, earning a better GPA, or surviving chemistry. Some are work related: finding your dream job or getting an apprenticeship. Because life is about more than just school or work, your goals can relate to anything—relationships, learning, or simply having fun.

Goals help us in many ways. Have you ever set a goal and achieved it? What did this experience teach you about achieving goals? Have you set a goal and *not* achieved it? Run through the experience in your mind. What got in the way that you have the power to change? What did you learn in the attempt? Failure, when well studied, is a great teacher.

Goals help clearly identify what you want to accomplish. They define how best to use your time to get what you want. Goals also help motivate you. The act of writing goals down makes them more real. Just saying you want to do something *someday* is not enough, since "something" and "someday" are not specific. Rarely do unclear goals get achieved. Change vague statements to clear, written-out goals. By making a clear statement such as, "In May of this year, I will jog a mile and not die or puke," you've articulated a feat you want to accomplish and given it a deadline.

Knowing your goals and setting milestones and deadlines to achieve them keeps you moving toward making them happen. A goal on a list is just an idea unless you put in effort to achieve it. When you achieve your goals, you feel better about yourself. Goal setting lets you discover and define how to spend your time, now and in the future. When you achieve your goals, life becomes more interesting, and you'll feel more in control of your destiny.

Goal Timelines

Different goals have different timelines and pacing. Your goal to submit an entry for a competition two weeks from now is paced faster than the goal to spend the summer teaching your cousins to swim. You may want to set three-month, six-month, or academic-term goals. Have papers to write or projects due? Listing what you must do daily, weekly, and monthly will help you achieve your goals without stomach-turning, last-minute drama.

Identifying long-term goals takes more time and thought. Goals reflect values. When mulling over long-term goals, you need to know:

- What is important to me?

- What do I most want to do with my time on earth?

These are not easy questions, but they are important to ponder. Some goals may change over time, while your desire to achieve others may become stronger. Some goals wind up unworthy of your time. Then once you've accomplished a goal, set another one.

PARACHUTE TIP

Get good at setting daily and weekly goals. Both give you the opportunity to practice working backward. Which three things are most important for you to get done today? If you have until 3 p.m. to accomplish your goal, what must you do by 9 a.m., by 11 a.m., and by 1 p.m.? If you need something done by Friday, what must you do each day before then to make that happen? Put your daily goals on a sticky note, your bathroom mirror, computer desktop, or set phone alarms. If you do daily or weekly goal setting for a few weeks, it will become a new skill. When your friends complain, "I didn't get much done this summer; I don't know where the time went," you'll know exactly where your time went—and you'll have a list of accomplishments to show for it.

> **"** *A goal is not always meant to be reached; it often serves simply as something to aim at.* **"**

—Bruce Lee, martial artist and actor

Accomplish Your Goals

A goal without a timeline is a wish. When you know your goals, it's important to plan how to accomplish them. Give your goals a deadline. To achieve a goal, you'll also need starting dates. Google calendars make it easy to look at six months or multiple years at-a-glance. Note on a calendar the dates by which you want your goals completed. Let's say that one of your goals is to attend a particular college or art or technical school. For each school, your to-do list might look like this:

1. Check school's website for admissions and application information and deadlines.

2. Do an internet search. Get the skinny on college applications and the institution itself.

3. Register to take the SAT (or other admissions tests).

4. Talk to a college admissions counselor about high school courses to take.

5. Register for those courses.

6. Take the SAT.

7. Visit the FAFSA website to complete student aid application: https://fafsa.ed.gov/

Goal Setting

Take a sheet of paper. Turn it so the long edge is horizontal, and fold it into four equal vertical columns. Draw a line near the top to create one row for column headings. Title the first column "What I hope to do in my life"; the next column, "Things I hope to do in the next one to three years"; the third column, "People have told me I should . . . "; and the last column, "If I were to die in six months, how would I want to spend my time?"

Set a timer for two minutes (or have a friend time you). Start with any column. Write down anything that comes into your head during those two minutes. After two minutes are up, set the timer for another two minutes and choose any one of the other columns. Repeat this exercise until you complete all four columns; in total, this should take just eight minutes.

Once you're done, read each column. What are your reactions to what you've written? Are there surprises? Were any sections more difficult to complete than others?

Take a look at that last column, "If I were to die in six months, how would I want to spend my time?" What activities did you include? Your list should reflect the things you value most—does it?

You probably have things you must get done in six months or face serious consequences (term papers and finals come to mind). But life needs fun, too. What are some personal goals you'd like to start or accomplish in the next six months? If you've gained new perspective on your six-month goals, revise the list to reflect that shift both in your personal goals and those related to school or career planning.

Before prioritizing your goals, let a few days pass. Identifying what you want to experience in your lifetime may stimulate other ideas. Add each of these ideas to the appropriate column, depending on the time frame of the goal. When your list feels complete, prioritize your list so your most important items appear first. Write two or three favorite goals from each list at the center of your My Parachute diagram (page viii). Does adding goals to your Parachute affect or change your career focus?

Goals are an important part of your Parachute. Having a certain job or career may be one of your goals, and it will certainly provide the budget to achieve goals that cost money. It's important that the work you do helps you achieve your most cherished goals.

While working through your to-do list, let's say you discover that you don't have to take the SAT, but you must prepare a portfolio for admissions. Your revised to-do list might look like this:

1. Do an internet search. Get the skinny on college applications and the institution itself.

2. Get explicit requirements for the portfolio from an admissions counselor at the college.

3. Ask an admissions counselor about portfolio requirements or high school courses to take to get better prepared.

4. Begin assembling a portfolio.

5. Complete a portfolio by the application deadline.

6. Fill out FAFSA.

A to-do list breaks your goal into manageable steps. If you make the steps too big, you may get discouraged. If the steps are just the right size, you'll keep moving toward your goal. If you find yourself avoiding your to-do list, that could be a sign you either don't really want to achieve this goal or the steps are too big. If one big step has you stuck, break it down into two or three smaller steps. Each time you complete a step, check it off. Completing a step is an accomplishment in itself, and each step you complete moves you closer to your goal.

Reevaluate Goals Often

As you move toward a goal—long-term goals especially—you'll gain new experiences and gather new information that will help you evaluate that goal. The things you learn while working toward a goal can be more valuable than achieving that goal. You might confirm that a particular goal is the right one for you, or you might revise it to include new ideas or new life directions. It's okay to let go of goals that no longer have meaning for you. Replace old goals with new ones that are more important to you.

If you find yourself setting but not achieving your goals, are you actually spending any time on them? Time spent on a task is directly linked to achievement. If you think you are too busy to work on achieving your goals, take inventory of how you spend your time, and see where you could carve out twenty to thirty minutes a week to work on a goal. Using a calendar app, you can make a colorful time chart. Use specific colors to indicate time spent in class, doing homework, working, volunteering, or in organized activities. Give your free time a different color.

Feel like you don't have any free time? Set your phone alarm for fifteen or twenty minutes, and when the alarm goes off, write down what you were doing during that time. Do this for every day for up to a week to get a good idea of how you spend your time, and to identify where you can divert time to working on your goals.

Hint: Most of your free time is spent on social media. The average teen spends seven hours and twenty-two minutes online every day. While some of that time may be spent doing homework, most is not. Use those twenty-two minutes to work on your six-month goals. Then turn your attention to longer-range goals.

Plan Backward

The best career development is done backward. Identify your goals and build out your strategy backward, from the future to the present. Write down each step from where you are, to where you want to be. Do the steps connect you to your ideal job? Are there gaps? For example, if an admissions counselor tells you that a certain major or certification will get you the job you want, verify that with employers. Once you know what training or education top employers want you to have, getting it becomes your goal. To get the qualifications you need, trace the steps backward from your goal to now. What must you do, and by when?

> 66 *If a student in junior high school wants to become a physician, it is worth knowing the important milestones she will have to clear to achieve her goal. Starting backward tends to help students become excited about the reward, but also unveils the important obstacles and work required to realize their ambitions.* 99
>
> —Anthony Hernandez, board president, Gina's Team, and the first in his family to graduate from college (Harvard)

PARACHUTE TIP

If you'd like to see how setting goals for yourself can help you bring about future success, but aren't sure how to make it happen, enlist the help of an adult you trust. With your goal coach, brainstorm ideas for a very short-term goal—say, thirty days from now. What do you need to do every day to achieve your goal?

A Tool for Life

Goal setting isn't something you do once. You'll find that the goals that interest you change over time. Setting goals and developing to-do lists for accomplishing them is a lifelong process. Knowing how to set and achieve goals is an important life tool. The goals you set and work toward shape your life.

CHAPTER 8

Social Media: The New Normal for Career Connection

You know social media. No doubt you've used social media since you were in middle school. What you may not know is social media can be a powerful tool for career exploration, information, and job hunting.

Social media has superpowers that can help you explore careers, meet people whose work interests you, uncover internships, and find job openings. You can also use social media to create an online job-search support group, follow companies you'd like to learn about and work for, create blogs about your interests, or share relevant career information.

In this chapter, we'll explore social media in the following ways: how to build a bulletproof web presence, connect with useful career information, expand your network, hunt for jobs, and set up a LinkedIn account—and stay safe while doing it.

A World of Possibility

Most teens and young adults know the details about very few jobs, and the same is true for older workers. Job descriptions on career information sites are broad and may be written by someone who has not actually done the job. Social media has expanded access to information exponentially. Different streams of information that would have previously taken months to assemble, can be found in a few days with social media.

The internet has unlimited potential for multiplying connections through web-based groups. In the mid-1960s, psychologist Stanley Milgram did a study that found we are all connected by an average of six people—proving it's a small world. This phenomenon is called "six degrees of separation." Thanks to social media, six has now shrunk to two, which means it's incredibly easy to be connected with someone in your chosen job or field. Be aware that the people closest to you often know the same people you do. This means that people farther out in your network have contacts you don't. Figure out how to get connected to those people. Now there's no excuse for not meeting living heroes, role models, or that one person you know you would love to ask, "How did you do that?" It's all in your approach, which needs to be respectful. You probably don't like being asked for a favor the first time you meet someone, so it's safe to assume others don't like it either.

REALITY CHECK

Most likely you have a personal social media account. This chapter is about how to create and use one to help you explore and find your place in the world of work. Putting together your online profile for career exploration and job hunting takes more thought, time, and attention than you might expect. The Discovery Exercises in this chapter might take a few weeks to finish. Get them done so you can take advantage of any opportunities you come across. If you want to keep your personal social media separate from an account for occupational exploration, make your personal account private.

Millennial author Dan Schwabel keeps his book *Me.2.0: 4 Steps to Building Your Future* up to date. Get the latest copy to learn how to build your brand.

Get Started: Create a Solid Web Presence to Build Your Brand

Over time, social media platforms come and go. Ever heard of MySpace? It was among the first generation of social media platforms. No matter the platform, the need for having one remains the same: to present yourself in a positive light and tell your story in such a compelling way that it attracts opportunities. Think out the image you want to project. It's easier to start out with a well-thought-out strategy for your online persona than to lose opportunities and have to do damage control. Make sure the image you project to the world is appropriate for your age, your educational and professional goals, and for public viewing.

There are dozens of blogs, tweets, and internet marketing impresarios sharing ideas about how to craft your brand (that's *you*, by the way). The old rule about having just one chance to make a good first impression takes on intense new meaning with social media. Almost weekly, there are stories of people who lost job offers or got fired because of something on their social media feed. Building your network with social media also lets you experience firsthand how small the world has gotten. Join any site or group associated with your job interests, and you may be contacted by people from all over the world. Make sure you're putting your best self forward.

- **YOU DON'T HAVE TO START FROM SCRATCH.** Ask friends, older siblings, coworkers, parents, or other adults you are close to if they have used social media sites for career exploration, information, or job hunting. If they have, you might want to ask for their help in setting up your profile, or ask to see their profiles as models. Check out the profiles of some of the gurus in your favorite fields or industries. What can you learn from how they present themselves?

- **WHAT'S IN A NAME?** On social media, the name you use can lead to opportunities found and lost. You want people to be impressed with your profile. Use your legal name, or variations of it, to create your social media profiles. No monikers—such as Leticia "Bunny" Brown, or Derrick "BadBoy" Jones.

- **DITTO FOR EMAIL HANDLES.** Create an email address appropriate for the business world. Your first and last name run together, first initial and last name run together, or name of your company if you've started a business. This is not the time to use a silly or risqué nickname.

- **CHOOSE A PICTURE WORTH A THOUSAND WORDS.** People looking up others on social media really, really look at pictures. These folks will make quick decisions about your character and competence based on what they see.

  Headshots are considered the most professional. Choose clothing and background colors that make you look good, not washed out. You want to create a neutral to positive image. No skin showing below your neck. Arms are covered. Young women can wear a blouse or dress and cardigan or jacket, and light makeup. Guys, white or blue shirts with or without tie. Sport coats are always acceptable. Look like the people who already have jobs in the industry you hope to work. Why so bland? Judge-y even? Because the person deciding whether to hire you, admit you to college, approve your scholarship, internship, apprenticeship, or other experience critical to your career development could be from another country, culture, ethnic or religious group far more conservative than you are. If your application is denied, you will never know why and never be able to rectify the situation.

- **USE LINKEDIN** to guide you setting up a profile. Google "LinkedIn for teens." LinkedIn isn't just for adults; high school and college students should also have a LinkedIn profile. People reviewing your applications for scholarships, internships, special programs or college will look for you on LinkedIn because it's just expected that ambitious teens will have one.

PARACHUTE TIP

Currently, Instagram, TikTok, Snapchat, and YouTube are the most popular social media sites among teens and young adults; Twitter and Facebook, not so much. Although no longer considered cool, don't overlook Facebook. From acrobats to zookeepers, from someone in your town to someone on the opposite side of the world, you can learn about jobs or a new place to live. Rather than take down your Facebook account, clean it up so it has a professional look, and use it frequently for career information and exploration.

The best pictures for your profile should support your brand and show your academic or occupational interests. You in a lab coat; tinkering in your robotics class; designing at your computer; wearing a company uniform or jacket; or putting a horse you've trained through its paces, for example. Change pictures every few months. Select images that shine a spotlight your interests and accomplishments.

To everyone: no gang style, no hand gestures, no sloppy pants. Remove large piercings of any kind anywhere on your face or head. You are not auditioning for *American Idol* (unless you are). Look like the professional who works in your chosen field.

REALITY CHECK

What does "professional" look like anyway?

Here are other ways to say "professional": expert, able, accomplished, masterful, polished, skilled, proficient, competent, practiced, trained, business-like, ethical, appropriate, fitting, correct.

Here are a couple of antonyms: amateurish and inappropriate. It is inappropriate, amateurish, and unprofessional, for example, to list your interests as partying and snogging; to display hand signs in your photos; and to post sexy or underdressed selfies.

Clean Up Your Act

Understand that the internet is forever. Some people have posted compromising images of themselves online that someday their grandchildren will see. Has that thought ever crossed their minds? Do they not care? Most adults have had a scrape or two in their youth that they'd prefer not to have revealed, much less circling the globe into infinity. With the Web, images sent out innocently can come back to hurt. Here's how to make sure that doesn't happen:

- **GOOGLE YOUR NAME.** Take a look at what hiring managers, owners of local stores, college admissions officers, scholarship committees, armed service recruiters, job recruiters, human resource personnel, and others will see if they look you up online. Remember, 90 percent of organizations considering you for a job or reviewing an application of any sort will look you up online. Seventy-nine percent of hiring professionals have nixed a candidate due to inappropriate content on their social media. Eighty percent of major companies monitor their current employees' social media. Nearly one out of three managers is a Millennial. Younger Gen Xers are media savvy too. If you ask someone for career information through a social media site, you can expect they will check out your online presence too. What will they find?

  Learn who else has your same name and what's on their social media sites. If someone else with your name has been arrested or has raunchy or racy pictures on their profile, you want to know and ward off potential rejections by making it clear that you are not that person. (Yes, I've even had to say, "No, I'm not that Carol Christen.")

- **DON'T LET FRIENDS NARROW YOUR OPTIONS.** If one of your friends is totally outrageous, posts extremely blatant prejudices, or likes to take unauthorized iPhone photos of you and other friends, block this person from posting on your career exploration social media accounts. Control who tags you in their photos.

- **USE BUSINESS ETIQUETTE IN ALL OF YOUR COMMUNICATION.** Your texts, IMs, and posts to friends' sites may be full of abbreviations, emojis, jokes, and colorful language. But when you contact people for career-related reasons, you must always maintain professional language and manners.

Why the emphasis on etiquette? Didn't that die out with hippies? In the business world, everyone's focus is on getting work done, and that means it's important to foster productive relationships of mutual respect with colleagues and customers.

The worlds of education and work are made up of people of all backgrounds, cultures, races, and countries who may or may not share your worldview, much less your sense of humor. Since each impression you make counts, knowing and using professional language and behavior keeps you from making mistakes you won't be able to correct.

Business Etiquette

Valuable employees demonstrate the following business etiquette:

1. Be respectful to your coworkers: stand straight, make eye contact, turn toward people who speak to you, smile, get to know people outside your department or cubicle, make personal phone calls during breaks, avoid office gossip and politics.

2. Maintain online etiquette: up to 30 percent of your day may be spent on email. Make your writing simple and clear, use standard English (capitalize proper nouns and the first word in a sentence; use punctuation and proper grammar), spell-check frequently.

3. Be accountable, especially if you make a mistake. Accountability requires honesty and integrity, and reflects upon your character.

4. Understand teamwork, and how you can be an asset to your team.

5. Jump at the chance to do a new task or project.

6. Follow your workplace dress code; even better, take yours up a notch.

7. Arrive early and prepared to work.

8. Filter your speech (do not use swear words).

9. Follow company rules and policies. If there's a handbook, read it! If not, observe others.

10. Brush up your table manners. Business lunches and dinners are part of work.

Virtual office etiquette and international business etiquette have their own specific rules. Search online to learn about them.

REALITY CHECK

Years ago, a frenemy of former Olympic swimmer Michael Phelps posted a picture of him smoking a bong that went viral. That betrayal cost Mr. Phelps a couple million dollars in endorsement contracts. Never trust anyone with a photo device in an embarrassing situation. Bullying of any sort is repugnant, but avoid any situation that could put your reputation at risk.

Design Your Web Presence or Rebuild Your Site

Designing your Web presence is a project that could take you up to six months to finish. Here are a few steps for getting started:

- Give some thought to the image you want to project.

- Clean up all your website pages or social media accounts so they look professional. Make informal social media accounts private.

- Do an online search of your name to see what potential employers will find.

- Pick appropriate photographs or avatars to represent you on different sites.

- Set up an email address on Google or Yahoo (LinkedIn has its own direct messaging system).

- Set profile privacy settings to allow communication only with approved connections.

- If you are fourteen or older, set up a LinkedIn account.

Set a date for when you would like to have each of the above steps completed, and write it down next to each item. As you finish each item in the list, write down its completion date. Comparing the two dates—your target deadline, and your completion date—will help you make better estimates of how long a project can take.

Keep a record of all your information someplace secure:

- What email addresses did you choose?

- What usernames did you choose?

- What are your passwords? Keep them private but remember where you put them!

Social Media Is an Excellent Career-Planning Tool

Social media works exceedingly well for gathering information about careers. It's an excellent way to find contacts; 80 percent of job seekers use social media. It's not that effective for getting hired; only 10 percent of job seekers get hired using social media. Like all tools, there are efficient and inefficient ways to use it. Below are some tips for applying what you've learned about career research and network building to the world of social media.

Reach Out for Career Information

Social media sites are great ways to get career information. YouTube videos can help you meet people and see skills in action. People who work at a place you might want to work, have jobs in a field you think would suit you, or live somewhere you'd like to know more about are just a few clicks away.

Through expanding your social network contacts, it's easy to connect with people who can answer your questions about fields, jobs, and organizations of interest to you. But be sure to do your homework first: read enough information about the person, company, job, or field that you don't take up a new contact's valuable time asking about basic information that you could have found online. Your questions should show that you've read and thought quite a bit about the topic or industry.

Help focus your social media searches by knowing:

- Who do you want to meet? You'll need to talk with people doing the job, then identify hiring managers.

- What information will help you expand your job options?

- What jobs best match your ideas about earning a good living?

- Do these jobs tend to be in a particular economic sector? Which one?

- Who are the top ten employers where you want live? Which ones have goals that you support?

- Who are the top ten people to watch in your field?

- What do you want to know from them?

- Where can you volunteer to get experience?

These are ideas to help you make a list of questions that you can ask others who share your interests. Tell your contacts you'd like their help getting a career question answered. Post the question. When what you want is information, you should get help quickly.

REALITY CHECK

Using social media sites to build a network of professional contacts may be the best job-search strategy of the twenty-first century.

Social Media Makes Finding Mentors Easier

Teens, young adults, and even adults without relevant work experience will rarely be hired beyond an entry-level job in their favorite fields. Entry-level jobs give you the opportunity to show what you can do for an employer. Once you know you want to stay in your current field, start laying the groundwork for moving on to your next job. Again, mentors can help you build a plan to get the education, experience, or training you need to build your career.

Successful adults often have mentors or coaches to guide their lives. Mentors can listen to your goals and help you communicate them. Mentors use their experience and contacts to maximize your options and guide you in creating a strategy for finding excellent job opportunities.

Know your next step or career goals but don't feel inclined to share those goals with the adults around you? If role models in your life are as rare as armadillos in Alaska, social media is a terrific way to meet people who can help. Let people know you follow them; read and comment on their posts. After a few exchanges, ask if they would be willing to give you some specific advice or answer a few—seriously, no more than three—questions. Don't be disheartened if they refer you to articles or other information they have already written. Use the links, read, comment, and send your thanks. If you still have questions, ask them. If you want to be able to check in with them periodically as a mentor, ask for that too. To succeed in the world of work, you'll need to be persistent and tenacious.

PARACHUTE TIP

If you'd rather be grounded for a month than to reach out to someone you don't know, practice with social media interest groups first. Can you find groups that align with your interests? In addition to finding interest groups on LinkedIn (see page 126), ask your career mentors if they know of websites or groups for your field or interests. Read posts and ask questions of the group. Making contacts and getting accurate job information is a survival skill that you will need to use over and over as an adult. As with all new activities, there's a learning curve; no one gets it right the first time. Even if you feel uncomfortable the first or second time, just do it. You'll get better.

Here's an example:

Fellow apiarists doing coding:

In Mumina Zymbraun's recent article on bee-bots, she noted some of the coding issues. However, she did not mention how code was developed using flower color to influence bee-bot pollination choices. Does anyone know how that was done?

Sincerely, Rebecca Gomez

Design and Build a LinkedIn Profile

LinkedIn is currently the premier social media site for business. Most ambitious employees, employers, recruiters, college admissions committees, successful entrepreneurs, and those who want to be successful entrepreneurs use LinkedIn.

In some countries, you can be as young as thirteen to set up an account on LinkedIn. In most English-speaking countries, including the United States, you must be fourteen to do so.

But isn't LinkedIn for older workers? Not anymore. LinkedIn is encouraging high school students to set up a profile, make contacts, and use those contacts to make career and higher education decisions. Potential employers will expect to find you there, while potential contacts will be impressed to see you there.

PARACHUTE TIP

Set up your LinkedIn Profile using this checklist provided by LinkedIn for students:

https://university.linkedin.com/content/dam/university/global

For more information about why you want to set up a LinkedIn profile as a teen and how to do it, read:

https://www.proresource.com/2020/04/
linkedin-for-high-school-students-get-started-now/

It will take time to set up your LinkedIn profile, so start now. One great advantage of LinkedIn is that you can correspond with your connections through LinkedIn messages—you don't have to share a personal email address. This feature gives younger teens (and their parents) the confidence that having a LinkedIn account is safe. However, once you start using LinkedIn to find an after-school or an entry-level job in your favorite field, you will need to have an email address so that employers may contact you directly.

Speaking of connections, it's time to build that list! Those who use LinkedIn like a boss recommend you have 500 contacts.

Build Your Contact List

But I don't have any contacts! Oh yes, you do. Everyone has between 150 and 250 relatives, extended family, friends, or acquaintances—including each of your friends. It's the people your friends know that can often connect you to the information you need. When you read phrases such as "leverage your LinkedIn account," what's being talked about is using your contacts to get a question answered, or asking your network to check with their contacts so you can get questions answered or meet a particular person.

Your first list of contacts is easy to put together, it's people you know. It's family, friends of your family, relatives, teachers of the subjects you'd like to use in your work, scout or club leaders, youth ministers, work supervisors, and others who managed you on volunteer projects. Ask them to connect with you on LinkedIn. Expand outward to people you don't know. Ask to connect with people whose books, magazine articles, or blogs you've read. Try to connect with heads of local, national, or even international professional associations. The list is endless. Go searching for these people on LinkedIn and ask them to connect with you. Not all of them will have LinkedIn profiles or connect with you, but many will say yes. Avoid using the impersonal greeting LinkedIn suggests, and write your own greeting instead. If it's someone you know but haven't seen in awhile, refer to shared experiences to remind that person who you are and how you met.

Find Groups to Follow

Whether it's an employer, an admissions officer, or a scholarship selection committee, the people who view your LinkedIn profile expect to see you connected to online communities or groups that reflect your interests.

Once you have your LinkedIn account set up, click on the Interests tab. Within LinkedIn, search each of these categories: People, Companies, and Groups. Scroll down and click on Groups. Find and join groups that align with your career or job interests. Read posts for awhile and get to know the group. Once someone makes a comment you like or have a question about, introduce yourself, ask to connect, and start a conversation.

Professors are always encouraging their students to use LinkedIn. If you build and use your LinkedIn profile now, you will practically be an expert by the time you graduate from high school.

PARACHUTE TIP

If you send a request on LinkedIn or other social-networking sites, always reply to every response you get. Blowing people off is a sure way to get blown off in the future. People who give you the name of a contact are putting their reputation with that person at risk. Regardless of your interest in the information they gave you, send a brief, polite follow-up message for every name you are given. You are thanking this person for their time, not necessarily for their information, and you never know when your follow-up will open a door. Those who don't follow up won't find many open doors.

Check Out University Pages

University Pages at LinkedIn were started so high school juniors and seniors could learn more about academic institutions they might want to attend. Through University Pages, you can find people's majors, where they work now, and how they feel about their time at a particular university or college. If you are thinking about getting a bachelor's degree but are unsure of what school you want to attend, once you've set up your LinkedIn profile, find the University Pages for the schools that interest you and start making contacts with alumni. The people listed on these pages have put their names up because they want to answer questions from students just like you. You may also be able to contact career center personnel and even professors to ask about educational recommendations and job prospects for potential majors.

Introducing yourself to alumni in your major or program when you graduate from college or university is expected as part of a successful job search. You can use them as part of your "where should I go?" research too. Before you pick a university, contacting current students or alumni from the departments you are considering can help you decide which educational institutions are better value. A mediocre department or program at a spectacular university won't do much for your employability. Contact a couple people in each program or major at each institution where you applied or have been accepted. (*Author's note:* My daughter did this, and it turned out the prestigious university did not have a prestigious department for her area of study. Had she not done this research, she likely would have started at Prestigious U, only to have to transfer to a school with a better department—which would have added a fifth year to her education.)

This post from Career Sherpa shows you how to find alumni through LinkedIn University Pages https://careersherpa.net/the-easiest-way-to-research-and-find -alumni-on-linkedin/

LinkedIn has yet to start similar pages for technical schools or community colleges, so you'll have to dig a bit for information on these schools. You can start by looking at your high school's Facebook page. You may be able to find alumni from your high school who went into a branch of service, technical training program, got a job, or attended a community college about which you are curious. Through Facebook, you may also be able to connect with your high school's booster club, which is made up of people who work or live in your community and want to help the school and its students. Attend a booster club or school board meeting and ask if you can have agenda time to announce that you'd like to meet people who (fill in the blank). Collect names, business cards, and email addresses. Kiwanis and Rotary clubs are big on helping teens and young adults, and often school principals and counselors are members. Ask yours if they will help you connect with service club members who do the work you want to do, are veterans of the branch of service you might join, or went to a certain school or training program.

Be sure to send a thank-you email to all new contacts who answer your questions, even if their information was not that helpful to you. You are thanking them for time spent on your behalf. Your gratitude will encourage them to help other high school students and young adults.

 DISCOVERY EXERCISE

Experiment with Twitter for Career Exploration

Set up a Twitter account for career exploration. Make a list of your ideas for using Twitter. Plan out your profile. Run your choice of headshots or avatar by a teacher or friend. What do you want to say publicly about yourself and your career search? Which privacy settings will you use on your site? Share this information with a trusted, media-savvy adult and ask for their suggestions too. The more thought you give to the details of your online presence before you hit "publish," the more quickly you can finish this step and get on to using your account to learn about careers.

Stay Safe Using Social Media

One upside of exploring careers on a site you're already on is that you are connected to people you trust. (If there are people you are connected to whom you do not trust, block them.) Friends will likely be able to connect you with people who have greater experience and more current information than what you've read so far. Asking questions of others who have gone down the path you are considering reveals details you might not have been able to find on your own.

Before posting, you need to carefully plan how to minimize any risk to yourself. For your safety, consider how much access you will allow to new contacts. What image of you will they see when they contact you? What should you reveal about yourself and your career search? Which privacy settings will you use to limit who sees this information?

Since many of your friends and classmates will also be using social media to get career information for their post–high school plans, consider asking a teacher if time can be scheduled for a class discussion about safely using social media and setting up positive profiles. If none of your teachers is social media savvy, find another adult who is. Listen to their suggestions for keeping yourself safe while using this powerful tool to access career information.

If, despite your best efforts, someone you're connected with online creeps you out, cease all contact and send all correspondence to your parents or another adult you trust. To minimize the likelihood of inappropriate contact, don't post your address. Only provide phone numbers or an email address after you've had a few exchanges with a new contact, their responses have been appropriate, and you feel using phone or email will make collecting information easier. Don't respond to anyone who bullies or harasses you, makes sexual innuendos, or comments too much on your appearance. Don't post inappropriate pictures (if your grandma wouldn't approve, it's probably inappropriate). Avoid meeting strangers in person, or behind closed doors. Make all appointments for information interviews at a business or public place. Zoom information interviews are ideal for safety. The world is full of wonderful and terrible people. May you meet far more of the former, and have a plan for your online presence that minimizes your chances of meeting the latter.

Job Hunting through Network Building

Using the same network-building protocol that you used for finding career information, you can also find job-shadowing opportunities, internships, volunteer work, training and education programs, and even jobs through social media.

Making a new friend adds one person to your network. To get enough information for a successful job hunt, you need access to dozens of people. Consistently over time, and in almost any field, the fastest way to get a job is by creating a network of eight to twenty people doing the work you want to do. Start by making connections through existing friends. Through social media, you can grow your job-search network very quickly.

Your contact lists should keep evolving as you go through the different stages of job hunting. A successful job hunt involves learning about the job, finding the best employers for those jobs, and starting a campaign to get hired. Some contacts will be great at alerting you to job openings. Others can teach you how to tell your story—the personal sales narrative that's necessary for a good interview. Do you know what it takes to move your career along? If not, this is another good question your contacts can help answer.

Here's how to finesse job hunting through social media:

- Don't ask a new contact for a job right away. Executives and hiring managers everywhere from high-profile to lessor-known companies, and even the local employers in your hometown, are asked for jobs all the time. You'll stand out if you *don't* ask.

- Post messages and questions to learn more about a company, a person, and what's happening in a particular job, field, or industry.

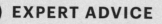 **EXPERT ADVICE**

Using Online Tools to Start (or Jump-Start) Your Career Path

By Patti Wilson, MA, founder of the Career Company
www.linkedin.com/in/pattiwilson

The internet is a vital hub of educational and career information, resources, opportunities, and contacts. It's also the main way that all companies, regardless of size, recruit talent. My favorite restaurant down the street uses Indeed.com to find new waitstaff. Urban Outfitters has elaborate online screens for new salespeople. Employers use multiple online platforms, including their own Web pages, and widely-known sites such as Linkedin.com, Indeed.com, and Glassdoor.com. Many local businesses also use local sites like Craigslist.com. And of course, they all use Google searches to find out more about promising job candidates.

Competition for entry-level jobs and internships continues to be strong. To stand out, a strong and professional Web presence is a given. Here are five tips you can use right now to give your career path a boost.

Own Your Name

It's never too early to buy your name as a URL address, aka: www.firstnamelastname. com. Grab it before somebody else does! (If dot com is already gone, try .net, .info, .biz, .me . . .)

You can also set up extra email addresses on Gmail and Outlook now to ensure that you have them when you need them later on in your work life.

Eventually you'll want to use your URL for a website, a portfolio of work, or a blog. Beyond college admissions staff, your personal URL raises your profile with recruiters and hiring managers as they find you in a Google search. Google's algorithms search by first and last name.

Aim to be found by a name search on the first page of Google after you graduate from college and start your career.

Protect Your Identity

Start managing your online privacy *now* to protect your reputation. It's crucial to selectively control who sees you, and where, online. You want only appropriate information about you to be found via name search.

Use Snapchat for sending texts and images that disappear after twenty-four hours, or an alternate name on Instagram for friends and family. Use your real name to create an instant visual or audio portfolio on Instagram and YouTube. On any site where you must use your real name, like LinkedIn, set your privacy settings to high and decide carefully who can see posts and who can connect with you. Your privacy settings should be set to provide no direct access to you via email, phone, or offline address. The exception to this is job sites where you enter your email address and phone number when applying for a position.

Never put down a full street address on an online resume—just your city and state, or a landline phone number will suffice.

Create a Big Digital Footprint

The first impression colleges and companies have of you can be enhanced by writing blog postings on Medium.com, posting articles on LinkedIn, and Amazon/Goodreads book reviews. By sharing your opinions and observations online, you continually build a brand. Be selective with the content and topics you choose, as you are building your long-term persona and reputation with every comment. *You can include links to articles and books that you have referenced in your resume.*

Hunt for Potential Career Ideas

A good place to start is by reading job postings from companies whose services you like and use in your daily life. These can lead to ideas for classes to take and majors to pursue. Dig into the career pages of multiple companies to learn about the career possibilities available.

Don't wait until you graduate. Start with the websites you frequent and expand from there.

Join LinkedIn.com Now!

LinkedIn's website presentation is low-key and professional. With nearly a billion members, it's the eight-hundred-pound gorilla in the room for finding and getting hired for jobs. One of the best things you can do for your future career is to join LinkedIn and put up a profile while you're still in high school.

There are sites similar to LinkedIn.com in Europe, including www.Viadeo.com in France and India, and www.Xing.com in Germany. Create your profile there if you are seeking an internship or full-time work outside the United States.

The awesome power of LinkedIn shows up on its college profile pages, where you can search for alumni by location, employment, and major. If you are trying to decide on a major or a university, contacting alumni from that school or major will help make your process easier. Requesting a brief conversation not only gives you the answers to your questions; it also expands your network of valuable contacts.

Set a goal to have 500 connections on LinkedIn by the time you graduate from college—they will be the support team for your job search.

- Introduce yourself and ask questions that can lead to a positive exchange.

- Get advice for ways to become more employable in your favorite fields.

- Once you have a good relationship with your contacts, you can ask more directly about job opportunities in the fields they have worked in or know about. Would they recommend you for such a job?

- Even better: if they are impressed with you and think you are competent, one or more of your contacts may bring up job opportunities on their own.

Now that you have constructed your business persona and know to use social media for career exploration and job hunting, you're ready to work on landing a great job.

All the work you've done in the earlier chapters of this book provides a foundation for this next important step. In Part One, you became a detective in your own life, finding clues to fill in your Parachute. In Part Two, you explored ways to continue the journey toward becoming happily employed by making the most of high school and higher education, and how to use tools like goal setting and social media.

Now we'll dive into the depths of job hunting. First in chapter 9, we explore concrete ways to make your job hunt more efficient, effective, and successful. Then we explore hiring interviews in chapter 10. Since many of you will find success in careers not yet imagined, in chapter 11 we'll explore career trends. Finally, we put the search for a wonderful job in the larger context of your whole life in chapter 12, and invite you to consider who you want to be, what you most want to do with your life, and how you can use your talents to make the world a better place to live.

❝ *Always be a first-rate version of yourself, instead of a second-rate version of somebody else.* **❞**

—Judy Garland, singer and actress

PART THREE

Land a Job You Enjoy, Create Your Ideal Life . . . and More

> 66 *I wish that someone had told me that success comes more easily if you are doing a job that you truly enjoy and not to pursue a career that seems 'safe' if it is going to make you miserable. People have said that forever. Apparently this needed to be pounded into my head.* 99

—Julie Porteous Leach, auditor, age 29

CHAPTER 9

Find Your Best Job Fit

Job hunting is both exciting and scary. The process becomes an adventure when you look at all the elements of your Parachute and say, "I wonder how these all come together in a job?"

With your Parachute finished, are you curious about jobs that will fit you? What are those job titles? Do similar positions exist in different fields? Knowing answers to these questions puts you ahead of most job-seeking young adults who seldom have a clue where they fit in the world of work. A set of overlapping circles is called a *Venn diagram*. The Venn diagram below shows you what you must do to find a job you will enjoy.

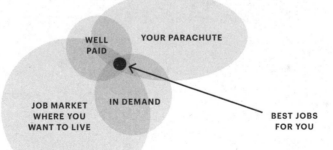

WELL PAID

YOUR PARACHUTE

IN DEMAND

JOB MARKET WHERE YOU WANT TO LIVE

BEST JOBS FOR YOU

REALITY CHECK

At times in your life, you may need to take a job that's good enough or barely okay—always try to find the best job you can in the labor market where you live. Finding a job you like takes the same amount of effort as finding a job you don't like. But if you don't like your job, you won't work hard enough to be a success. In the business world, it's the people who do A- and B-level work who get promoted.

PARACHUTE TIP

Five steps to a great job for you:

Step 1: Conduct information interviews.
Step 2: Get necessary qualifications and relevant experience.
Step 3: Cultivate contacts and create networks of people holding that job and hiring for it.
Step 4: Research organizations that have the jobs you want.
Step 5: Design and execute a campaign to get the job you want.

Repeat these steps with each job target in every field that fascinates you. A good job search has three related job targets.

Five Steps to a Job You Love

Let's go through the steps—some of which you'll recognize from earlier chapters—that will help you land a job you'll love . . .

Step 1: Conduct information interviews.

Too many people make their job search harder by starting in the wrong place: they try to get hiring interviews before knowing their best skills, the situation with the job market, what jobs they want, or how to present themselves. But you've already done the exercises in part one and identified three potential jobs that match your Parachute. Ready to look for your first full-time job in your preferred field? The first step is to do lots of information interviews. You learned the basics of interviewing for information in chapter 4 and the fundamentals of social networking in chapter 8. Now you'll build on those basics.

Remember, information interviewing shouldn't be complicated or intimidating. Again, it's just a conversation with another person about a shared interest or enthusiasm—in this case, a particular job or career. You'll ask questions, but spend most of your time listening. Let the people you're interviewing tell you their stories about how they came to do the work that interests you. Soon you'll know . . .

- More about the industry or field

- Common salaries for this work.

- Whether this is a good career choice for you.

- Employers who hire people to do this work.

- How to present yourself to get hired.

- If you need further qualifications.

- Names of jobs that you had no idea existed.

Information interviews will reveal whether or not your best skills match the most common requirements for a particular job, and how much the work overlaps with your interests. Before you ask people to talk with you, read several descriptions of that job, field, industry, or career. You will ask better questions, be a better listener, and the information you collect will make more sense. For each person with whom you have an information interview, use Google or LinkedIn to see what you can learn about them. What you read about an interviewee's background, experience, education, or current position will help focus your questions. Also, your interviewees will be impressed (maybe even flattered) that you took the time to research them.

Basic Information Interview Questions

- What do you do?

- What are three to five of the most common tasks or activities you do each day? What skills do you use doing those tasks? Do you mind the repetition?

- How long have you been doing this work?

- How did you get into this work?

- What kind of training or education did you need for this job? Do you mind if I ask how much it cost?

- What do you like about your job? What don't you like about your job?

- What are the main challenges in this industry?

- Will this job exist in three to seven years? (You need to know this about the jobs that interest you, especially those that require training. Is the training transferable to other jobs?)

- What do you see happening in this field in the next five to ten years? Will climate change, AI, or robotics impact this job? How?

- What is your ultimate career goal?

- What is the starting salary in this job or field? What is the salary range with three to six years' experience?

- Do you have any additional comments, suggestions, or advice?

- Can you give me the names of two or three other people who do this same work?

The goal of this first step is to find and talk to people who have jobs or careers that interest you. (These interviews are *in addition* to ones you may have done earlier, in high school, when you were just beginning to research jobs and careers.) Talking with people gives you a reality check for what you've read or heard about a job. If you don't talk to anyone before making an occupational choice, you are making that choice based on hearsay (which is as accurate as gossip), your own fantasies about that work, or how the media has portrayed that kind of job. The point of doing these information interviews is to find jobs that match your Parachute. The job that matches best becomes your first job target, the job that matches next best becomes your second job target, and so on. Try to find at least three kinds of jobs or careers that overlap with your Parachute. Having three job targets increases the likelihood of success.

PARACHUTE TIP

Never underestimate the value of thanking someone for talking with you. Your name might be forgotten, but your gesture will lodge in memory under "that nice kid who sent me a thank-you note." To review the basics of writing thank-you notes, see page 59.

Step 2: Confirm qualifications and relevant experience.

General descriptions of the work you want to do usually includes necessary education, training, or experience. Don't make assumptions. Check out these requirements with your information interviewees. The education, training, or experience specific employers and hiring managers want can be very different from generic career information. Knowing what your top employers want helps you save time, money, and needless frustration.

Step 3: Cultivate contacts and create networks.

The people you meet through information interviews become contacts and part of your career network. You already have a personal network of friends, family, and other people you have met; a professional or work network is necessary too. Both networks help your job search. Keep in touch with your contacts. Send annual updates about your life or career. You can use an online calendar to remind you to reach out to your contacts. Show interest in their lives as well. Has someone you haven't seen in a long time ever asked you for a favor, then dropped you again? Did you feel used? Most people in your professional network would feel the same. Just as preventative maintenance keeps your car running well, treating your contacts well keeps your networks healthy.

Contacts you have good relationships with become your eyes and ears on the ground. They may hear about job openings before they become public and alert you to those opportunities, and they may even put in a good word for you.

Keep contact information of people you meet—names, phone numbers, and email and mailing addresses—because you may need to access them in the future. You can create a career group in a contact app, or save this information in an online document or on your computer.

You can ask for people's contact names from:

- Family—immediate and extended

- Friends, and parents of friends

- Friends on Facebook or similar social media sites

- Neighbors

- School guidance counselors or club sponsors

- Teachers or professors

- Coworkers and bosses (past and present)

- People you've met through temporary or volunteer work

- Supervisors of volunteer or school projects

- Mentors or people you've job shadowed

- People you've met through information interviews

- Your pastor, rabbi, mullah, youth-group leader, or other members of your spiritual community

- Members of community-service organizations (such as the Lions, Kiwanis, Rotary, Soroptimists, American Association of University Women, and Boys & Girls Clubs)

- People you meet in line at the movies, grocery store, or on vacation

Ask each person if they know someone who does the job you hope to do, if they know someone who works in that field, or if they know someone working at a particular company or business. If you continue to get two or three names from each person you interview, you'll soon know what's happening with the jobs you want in the town you want to live.

66 *I wish I would have asked more questions about the future of architecture before I decided to become an architect. If I had asked older architects what changes they saw coming to the field, I think I could have anticipated some of the frustrations I'm now having with my profession.* **99**

—Scott J. Smaby, award-winning architect

Step 4: Research organizations of interest.

Have you done enough information interviews to prioritize your job targets (step 1)? Have you gotten the needed qualifications to be a strong candidate for hire (step 2)? Have you cultivated contacts to create a good-size network of people who do the work you want to do or work in fields that fascinate you (step 3)?

If you've done the first three steps, now it's time to find out what organizations hire people for your ideal job, in a location where you want to live. If the same job is available in different work environments, this round of information interviews will help you decide which organizations have the best work environment for you. In 2021, hiring executives started calling work environments "corporate culture ecosystems." It makes sense, considering animals thrive—or don't—in different ecosystems; the same is true for you. You are looking for an employment ecosystem that supports your ability to do your job well. Each information interview gives you more details about the work environment (boss, coworkers, culture, workspace) you can choose between employers. Use these details to create a prioritized list of ten employers for whom you'd like to work.

Building on your information interviews, you will now research these organizations more thoroughly. In addition to a general internet search, you can:

- Visit company, field, and industry websites.

- Look through old newspaper and periodical archives to find written information on the organizations.

- Talk to people who currently or used to work for organizations you're interested in. Also, talk with competitors (if this is a business) or people at similar agencies (if this is, for example, a nonprofit agency).

- Talk to the suppliers or customers of a business, or a particular department of a corporation.

- Ask for information from business leaders in your community, the local chamber of commerce, private industry council, or the state employment office.

When you contact people who currently or used to work for an organization, you'll want to get answers to the following questions about that organization (some of which are difficult to ask directly, so be very tactful):

- For what product or service is the organization best known?

- What goals are they trying to achieve? Are they achieving their goals? (Many organizations have mission statements. Read them!)

- What are their needs, problems, and challenges?

- What kind of reputation does the company have within the industry?

- How do they treat their employees?

- Which companies are growing? Which ones are shrinking? Beware of the latter!

Why do step 4? Employers get really irritated with interviewees that haven't researched the company (it's kind of like telling someone you're dating that you're not that into them). This step helps you avoid irritating the person interviewing you, increasing your chance of getting hired by a company for whom you have real enthusiasm. The more enthusiastic you are about working for Company X, Y, or Z, the more likely you are to present yourself as an excellent candidate during a hiring interview.

As you learn more about these organizations, some places will seem more appealing to you—that's exactly what you want to find out. After you've completed your research, you'll know which organizations hire people for your ideal job or career, and which work environments fit you best.

Step 5: Begin a campaign to get the job you want.

From your research in step 4, choose the top five places you want to work, and for each one identify the person who has the power to hire you. In a small business, the hiring manager might be the owner. In larger businesses, department managers conduct the hiring interviews. Reach out to the person who has the hiring power and ask for a twenty-minute appointment. Be direct. Tell this person you'd like to discuss how well your strengths match the job. (No, there doesn't have to be an opening.) About 65 percent of those you call will make an appointment with you.

Before your appointment, review your Parachute. Do any of the skills stories you wrote showcase how you've used the skills needed for this job? Rehearse how these items connect to the job you want. Saying important points out loud beforehand makes it easier to say them during the interview. Make an outline of everything you know about this job, the organization, and the person interviewing you. Ask questions about their needs and be ready to talk about how your skills, training, education, experience, and enthusiasm for this work can meet those needs and make you an outstanding employee. Keep your focus on what you can do for them. Employers already know what they can do for you.

If there's a company you want to work for and you haven't learned the name of the person who has the power to hire, use all your networks to get the information you need.

If no employment offers come from the first five organizations you targeted, select five more that have the jobs and work environments you want. Keep researching organizations, expanding the number of people in your network, talking with them, and asking for hiring interviews until you receive a job offer—or three.

66 *If you make ten inquiries and everyone says no one's hiring, expand your geographic boundaries, or change your target field.* **99**

—Marty Nemko, career coach and author of *Cool Careers for Dummies*

PARACHUTE TIP

Trying to get a job you won't like isn't necessarily easier than going for want you want. Two facts make this true:

- You will think of all sorts of excuses not to go hunting for a job that doesn't interest you.
- You will be in competition with people who think this job—the one you don't want—is their ideal job. Their enthusiasm will impress an employer. Your lack of enthusiasm will not.

Job-Search Basics

Now that you know the five steps to finding the job you want, let's take a closer look at some basics that will support and guide you.

What You Need for a Job Search

Because you aren't in control of other people's actions or decisions, the job hunt can feel frustrating. Creating, organizing, and storing your career-planning and job-search materials for quick retrieval makes you feel more in control. Here are some things you'll need for your job search:

- A desk or table. If not available where you live, a library or coffeehouse will do.

- Some way of storing, organizing, printing, and retrieving information you gather. This can be online, in a milk crate, or in a three-ring binder. Secure your work safely.

- A secure and reliable way of getting phone messages from employers and other contacts. Make sure you clearly state your first and last name in your outgoing greeting. Your recorded greeting should be business-like—no "Waz up at da tone." Your voicemail could be an employer's first impression of you—make it a good one. You may also want to mention your job search in your outgoing message. Here's a sample message:

> "Hi, this is Jessica Wong. I'm sorry I can't take your call right now. Please leave me a message after the beep. I'm currently looking for work in accounting at a hospital or large medical office. If you know of any leads or contacts for me, be sure to mention that too, along with your phone number. Thanks a lot." (This advice is not for someone who is currently working but hasn't told their employer they are job hunting.)

- An email address that you can check at least daily. Make sure your address is business-like; some form of your name should do. Many public libraries provide access to computers, the internet, and email for people who don't have them.

- A LinkedIn profile or other professional online Web presence where you can post your resume, list your accomplishments, gather recommendations, and so on (see chapter 8 for tips).

- Reliable transportation, for interviews and commuting to work once you are hired.

- Appropriate interview clothes. Observe how people are dressed at the places where you want to work. When you go for an information or hiring interview, wear clothing that's a little more formal than the way the employees dress. If you're on a tight clothing budget, some local community organizations provide good interview clothes for free or low cost.

The Best Ways to Look for a Job

COMMON METHODS	EFFECTIVENESS RATE	
Asking for job leads from friends and family	33%	
Going to see employers to sell yourself, vacancy or not	47%	
Doing the above in a job-search group	84%	
Being a job detective*	86%	

*A "job detective" follows the strategies used in this book: doing research on oneself, finding jobs that match skills and interests, identifying which places of employment have those jobs, determining who has the power to hire new staff, and getting a meeting with that person. The success rate of the job detective method is twelve times higher than just sending out resumes.

Tips for Savvy Job Searchers

Once you have what you need for your job search, the following techniques and suggestions will jump-start your progress:

- **SEARCH FULL-TIME.** Which means at least five to six hours a day, at least four days a week. The more time you spend actively looking for a job, the quicker your job hunt will go. Time spent doing information interviews, strengthening your network or revising your Parachute all count as job-search activities.

- **PROTECT YOUR JOB-SEARCH TIME.** If family and friends see that you're serious about devoting five or six hours a day to your job search, they should honor the time you put into finding the job that's right for you. If they don't, learn to say no.

- **REMEMBER THAT MANY VACANCIES AREN'T ADVERTISED.** Seventy-five to eighty percent of open positions aren't listed or published. Doing information interviews and letting people know what type of position you're looking for will increase your odds of finding unadvertised vacancies.

- **MAKE LOTS OF PHONE CALLS AND SEND LOTS OF EMAILS.** Keep at it until you've lined up at least two employers who will meet with you each day of the week (even if they have no current openings).

- **PRACTICE YOUR PITCH.** Create a twenty- to thirty-second pitch stating your name, the work you seek, and two or three of your best skills. Be able to add relevant job information about yourself in fifteen-to-twenty second sound-bites. Practice your pitch out loud until you can say it smoothly. You'll use this pitch over and over again when people ask you, "What are you looking for?"

- **TARGET SMALL ORGANIZATIONS.** Small businesses employ 97 percent of US workers and have fewer gatekeepers. If possible, begin your job search with organizations that have no more than twenty-five employees.

- **BE PREPARED TO GIVE REFERENCES.** Employers want to know about your reliability and personality. Think about whom in your network might be willing to provide a positive reference. Get written references before you start your job search.

- **VOLUNTEER AT LEAST ONE DAY A WEEK.** You can get great experience, make new contacts including possible references, and maintain your self-esteem while job hunting if you volunteer at a school or community event, nonprofit organization, local business, or place of worship.

PARACHUTE TIP

When's the best time to call?

Job hunters have reported that they have success reaching employers or hiring managers in person at the following times:

- First thing in the morning and last thing in the afternoon
- Fridays right before and after lunch

Resumes: Traditional and Visual

Readers who have written skills stories, filled out a Parachute, done some information interviews, and have had a few paid or volunteer jobs will find writing a resume fairly easy. Writing a resume is easier when you have lots of material about yourself and the work you want to do. A company with more than a couple dozen employees is likely to ask for a resume. Because many employers expect you to furnish a resume (even if you are directed to apply at their website), it's good to know how to create one.

There are four kinds of traditional (or written) resumes: chronological, functional, a combination of the two, and targeted. A chronological resume starts with your most recent work history and goes backward. Since teens don't usually have several jobs in their hoped-for career field, this format doesn't work well for most high school students. A functional resume focuses on skills and experience relevant to the job one wants. A combination chronological and functional resume highlights relevant experience first, and job history second. A targeted resume is customized for a particular employer and specific job—nearly all the resumes you write should be targeted. Targeted resumes highlight the skills, experience, classes, and training that show you are qualified for a specific job. Gone are the days of carefully typed resumes printed off by the hundreds; top employers expect targeted resumes. They know how easy it is to adapt your experience to a targeted resume using a word processing app. When you use a generic resume, an employer will think you didn't care enough to spend time modifying your resume. This will not help you get hired.

Visual Resumes

Visual resumes can be infographic, a slide presentation, short video, or photo collage. They are often expected in creative fields such as marketing, advertising, any kind of design from clothing to websites, architecture, and journalism. Visual resumes demonstrate your ability to create visually engaging content or show you can put together a compelling visual story. The people you have information interviews with can tell you whether a written or visual resume will help you stand out when applying for jobs in a particular field. If you talk with creative types, ask which kind of resume they used, and if you can see theirs.

You can conduct an online search to learn more about and see examples of the different kinds of traditional and visual resumes. Even better, when doing information interviews with people who have the jobs you want, ask if they will share their resume with you. You can get ideas for your own resume from looking at those of people who've gotten successfully employed doing what you want to do.

Resume format for teens:

Name	Resume for (fill in job title at business name, apprenticeship, volunteer position at . . . , or other opportunity)
Email	
Phone number	
High School*	
GPA (if 3.0 or higher)	

*Use if you are applying for an opportunity through your high school or one available only to students in your school district

What comes next is whatever qualifies you most for the job or opportunity you seek. This could be a particular class, several courses, training, certification, experience, volunteer work, a job, hobby or extracurricular activity. Use headings such as Relevant Experience, Relevant Activities, Relevant Courses, or Work Experience.

Example: Rafael was having a hard time getting an interview for a job that required physical fitness, making split-second decisions, being persuasive, taking risks, confidence, and a high level of competitiveness. Ditching traditional resume format (name, work experience, education), he used the heading "Relevant Activities" immediately under his name and listed two extracurricular activities. The first was winning a state wrestling championship and placing nationally. The second was winning a statewide competition as part of his debate team. He used the combined format (chronological and functional) for the rest of the resume and got an interview.

Have more history that shows how well qualified you are? Including paid or volunteer work, classes, training, or other experience in your resume shows you can do the work you seek. Use relevant headings to keep the information organized for readers.

Jobs (paid or volunteer) to show employers you have a work history. (Choose no more than three examples that have similar skills to the job you want.)

Other Interests, Hobbies or Extracurricular Activities

Your resume should fit on just one page. Be sure to convert your Word document to a PDF so the formatting doesn't get wonky. You should never include your physical address on a resume. After you send it off, you have no control over who sees it. If a job, scholarship, or other opportunity is available only to whose living in a certain town or area, include the name of your town, state abbreviation, and zip code. When you get hired, you will need to supply your mailing address for payroll and tax purposes.

Some Truths About Resumes

- Resumes are not an effective job-search tool for adults. They're even less effective for younger workers. Resume means history. If you don't have a history of doing the work you are now searching for, a traditional paper resume is not going to be much help.

- Your resume may not have the right words to get past a company's resume-screening algorithm. Another reason to talk with people doing the work you want to is that they can tell you which words might be magic.

- Rarely does someone reading a resume spend more than ten seconds doing so.

- Traditional resumes focus on past work history, which is useful only if your work history supports your next job goal (for instance, if you're changing jobs but staying in the same field, or changing fields but staying in the same job).

- People depend too much on a resume to get them a job. Never defer starting your job hunt until you have the perfect resume—it doesn't exist, and you might not need it. Spend time reviewing your best skills and strengths for the job. Think about stories from your experiences that show how you can use your abilities to the employer's benefit. Get out and meet people doing the work you want to do.

- You don't need a resume to start information interviews. If someone you interview asks for your resume, use what you learned to create a targeted resume and send it along with your thank-you note.

- If you've never done a serious job hunt, you need to get to know the job market where you live or hope to live. If it's been over a year since you have looked for work, you need to familiarize yourself with the current job market. If after a dozen information interviews, you find you need a resume, you'll write a much better one.

- If someone says, "Send me your resume," get their contact information or business card. Then, give them your pitch (about thirty seconds of information about you, why you want the job, and your most compelling qualifications). Why? Because when they get your resume, you want them to remember you as a competent, enthusiastic job seeker, not just a name on a piece of paper.

> 66 *Don't confuse life and work. It is much easier to write a resume than to craft a spirit.* 99
>
> —Anna Quindlen, writer

True story: an engineer went to a job fair after hearing a recruiter for the company she wanted to work for would be there. She handed over her resume and started counting. When she got to one-thousand-three, the recruiter handed her resume back to her and told her she wasn't qualified for the job. She realized that if the recruiter had spent three more seconds reading her resume, they would have seen her best experience linking her to the work she wanted. At the time, she was one of a very small number of engineers globally with experience in infrared aviation technology. She knew she was uniquely qualified for the job. She was so irritated with the recruiter that she searched through her contacts until she found someone who could introduce her to the department hiring manager. Ultimately, she got the job.

While it's great to get your resume in front of the person with the hiring power, getting hired is more likely to happen if *you* are in front of them.

PARACHUTE TIP

Do you know of someone who is looking for work too? You'll be more persistent, uncover more leads, and have more fun with a job-search buddy.

Take Care of Yourself

A job search can be very demanding. It can wear down even the most positive person. To deal with this:

- Don't focus on your job hunt being over. Instead, keep track of all the tried-and-true techniques you use. Create a chart to record how many phone calls, information interviews, hiring interviews, or new contacts you make each day. Higher numbers mean that you're conducting an effective job search. Expect a search for a career path job to last six to twelve months—and if it takes less time, rejoice!

- Create an "advisory board" for your job search: up to five people who can meet with you individually or as a group. Zoom is ideal for both. During your job search, meet once a month with people are supportive, know a lot about the industry or field you want to work in, are very good at getting jobs they want (perhaps you even met them while doing information interviews), and can give informed suggestions. Your advisory board members can send important information your way and keep your spirits up.

- Take care of your physical body too. Eat right, get enough sleep, drink less caffeine and more water, and avoid negative people. Bad habits negatively impact how you look and feel. Exercise, meditate, listen to motivational podcasts, see good friends, and watch movies that make you laugh and give you hope. If there are other things you enjoy doing that help you take care of yourself, incorporate them into your routine. Even going for walks reduces stress and helps you solve problems.

A job hunt can be very rewarding, but rarely is it easy. It demands physical, mental, and emotional energy. A successful job search takes dedicated time. Be gentle with yourself in the process. No one is expected to do everything right the first time.

> **"** What accounts for the difference between greatness and mediocrity? Extraordinary drive. **"**
>
> —Benjamin Bloom, author of *Developing Talent in Young People*

Ten Incredibly Common Job-Hunting Mistakes Newbies Make

- Thinking you must do this all by yourself
- Spending too little time on your job search (if you're unemployed, aim for six hours a day)
- Continuing to use techniques that aren't working
- Being financially unprepared for how long the job search really takes (budget for at least nine months)
- Ignoring successful techniques because "that's just not me"
- Having only one job target

- Limiting your job search to what's advertised rather than learning about unadvertised vacancies through information interviews

- Giving up too easily and too soon

- Thinking someone else will do this for you

- Starting in the wrong place. Don't seek employment interviews before you are ready to be brilliant in them. Treat the job hunt as a job, not a game.

Have you made any of the mistakes above? The job-search strategies and techniques you've learned in other chapters of this book will help you avoid fruitless efforts. Knowing what and what *not* to do will put you way ahead of less determined job hunters.

PARACHUTE TIP

The most effective—and least used—job-search strategy is to know ten to twelve people who do exactly the work you want to do, or who are employed in your target industry. They will hear of openings before you do. Twelve people are twelve sets of eyes and ears helping you with your job search. Imagine all the openings you could learn about if your network reached forty contacts!

 Nobody in life gets exactly what they thought they were going to get. But if you work really hard and you're kind, amazing things will happen. I'm telling you, amazing things will happen.

—Conan O'Brien, talk show host

CHAPTER 10

Hiring Interviews: The Scoop

The best reason to know effective job-search techniques is that you'll use them frequently during your money-earning years. Researchers speculate that people your age will be in the workforce sixty years and have a score of jobs. Time will tell!

You're ready for hiring interviews if:

- You've talked to between six and twelve people in the field or job you want.

- You've verified through reading and conversations that this work fits you and your qualifications.

- You've compiled a list of twelve to fifteen favorite employers.

- You know the names and have researched the hiring managers at the top five places you want to work.

- Your experience proves you have the skills needed in the jobs you want.

Goal: Get Good Enough at Interviews to Enjoy Them!

A hiring interview is simply a conversation focused on a specific job. But hiring interviews can be stressful. They're often compared to blind dates. Too often people go to interviews without knowing anything about their "date"—the interviewers and the company, organization, or agency where they are interviewing. Employers' two biggest gripes are interviewees who don't show up (what's with that?), and those who have done no research about the company. Don't make either mistake. The job hunters who stand out know about the work to be done **AND** the organization. You want to stand out! Everyone likes to be flattered. Knowing about the organization where you're interviewing is a sincere form of flattery. Saying things such as "I can't believe this company started in 2006 with just two people" will likely get a check in your favor and a good story from your interviewer with immediately useful information about them, the company, and perhaps the job you want. Learn as much as you can about the job you want and each organization that interests you. The more prepared you are, the better your interviews will go.

Don't expect your interviewer to make a connection between what's on your resume or cover letter, and your ability to do this job. Your resume is like a movie script, and your interview is the movie that brings the script to life. You must speak to your interest in and experience for this job in a way that shows how qualified you are to do it. Young people are often surprised how hard they have to sell themselves in an interview, even when the interviewer knows them and their previous work.

Imagine that you are an employer interviewing two applicants for one job. The first candidate seems either scared or bored. Her answers are brief. When asked why she wants the job, she replies that the pay is good and it's an easy commute. The other applicant begins by thanking you for the interview, then tells you about the classes she has taken to prepare for this work, and the internships she's done to hone her skills. When asked why she wants the job, this applicant answers that it's because of the company's great reputation. She says while she hopes you'll hire her, she will keep applying for similar jobs if she doesn't get an offer because it's what she loves and believes she is meant to do. Which applicant would you hire?

It takes young people nine information interviews before they feel comfortable enough to do them well. Assume you will have to do just as many hiring interviews before you get good at being interviewed. If your career center doesn't do mock interviews, ask adults or friends you trust to put you through interview scenarios, common questions, and to check out your handshake. It shouldn't be too strong or too weak. COVID caution: check with each person if they want to shake hands, bump elbows, or stay physically distant. Frequent practice of interviewing techniques keeps you focused, breathing, and thinking clearly even when you're stressed.

Hiring interviews are a lot easier if you've done information interviews. Through talking with people who have the job you want, you know the issues and challenges facing the industry both in general, and in this particular job. You may have butter-flies in your stomach during hiring interviews, but don't panic—you've talked with people about this type of work before. Your interviewer wants to know what you can do for the company; you want to tell your interviewer all that you can do for the company. A hiring manager wants evidence that you can use your education, training, and talents to help the company achieve its goals. The more homework you've done about yourself, the job, and the needs of the organization, the easier it is to ask and answer questions about the job. When the conversation flows, your interviewer gets a positive impression of you and your abilities. This makes hiring interviews more pleasant for each of you.

Before Your Interview

Before your interview, think about these two questions:

1. What do I still need to know about this job at this organization?

2. What information do I need to communicate about myself?

Listen for opportunities to learn what you need to know about the organization, and communicate your best qualifications. Do you sound convincing?

Common Interview Questions for Entry-Level Positions

1. Why are you interested in this job?

2. What are some of your favorite and least favorite classes? Why?

3. What do you know about this company?

4. How would you assess your writing and communications skills?

5. Describe a time when you disagreed with a coworker or classmate.

6. What (experiences, job, class work) has best prepared you for this job?

7. How would past managers or teachers describe you?

8. What are your strengths and weaknesses?

9. What activities do you do outside of school and work?

10. Have you worked on a team? How was that?

11. Have you ever taught a concept to a coworker or classmate?

12. How do you respond when someone critiques your work?

13. What are your long-term career goals?

14. How do you handle deadlines?

Visit this website to get flashcards to help you answer interview questions like those above:

https://www.wayup.com/guide/top-20-entry-level-job-interview-questions-and-answers/

No matter what questions your interviewer asks you, they will likely be from one of these five categories:

- Why are you here?

- Do you have the skills, knowledge, and experience we need?

- Can I afford you?

- What kind of a person are you? Do I want you working for me and representing our program, department, or company?

- What distinguishes you from nineteen other people who can do the same tasks that you can?

Your interviewer is afraid of making a poor hiring choice. If you know the fear behind the question, you can pick examples of your skills, experience, and suitability to address these fears.

PARACHUTE TIP

Brian McIvor is a highly skilled international career consultant who is also well trained in the Parachute process. You can access his free materials for improving your hiring interview techniques at: https://www.brianmcivor.com/welcome-to-the-interviewing-zone/

During Your Interview

Personnel professionals tell us that many interviewers make up their mind about you in the first half-minute of the interview. They spend the remaining time looking for reasons to justify their decision. It's not the technical questions that get applicants eliminated. Employers consistently report that these three factors most often influence your interviewer's first impression of you:

1. Were you on time for the interview?

2. Did you look the interviewer in the eye as you greeted them?

3. If offered, what was the quality of your handshake? Theirs?

What Interviewers Notice

A detailed study done by Albert Merhabian, PhD, at UCLA a couple of years ago revealed some surprising things about what interviewers pay attention to. It turns out that interviewers are preoccupied with nonverbal communication, and making sure it matches with what the interviewee is saying. If it doesn't, they're less likely to hire that applicant!

PERCENTAGE OF ATTENTION:	FOCUSED ON:
7%	**WORDS** Choose your words carefully. In three different ways, explain the skills, experience, or training that most qualify you for this job.
38%	**VOICE QUALITY** Don't have too much caffeine before an interview. If your voice tends to get high-pitched when you're nervous, take a thermos of warm water with you and have some sips before your interview starts.
55%	**NONVERBAL CUES** (Handshake, posture, what you do with your hands, nervous mannerisms, eye contact, and so on.) Don't always look your interviewer straight in the eye. This can be seen as threatening. Alternate direct looks with looking past their ear, slightly above the head.

During the interview, an interviewer is assessing your attitude. The way you conduct yourself in the interview gives a lot of clues as to what type of employee you'll be. An interviewer will quickly judge whether you are . . .

- A pleasant person to be around—or not.

- Interested in other people—or totally absorbed with yourself.

- At peace with yourself and the world—or seething with anger beneath a calm exterior.

- Outgoing or introverted.

- Communicative or monosyllabic.

- Focused on giving—or only on taking.

- Anxious to do the best job possible—or just going through the motions.

Your interviewer notices whether you project energy, or expend only minimal effort to engage. Do you exude curiosity, or a sense of sullenness? To employers, your attitude is more important than your skills, because it signals how hard you're willing to work and whether you can work well with other people. Employers will hire someone with fewer skills and a good attitude before they'll hire a more experienced person with a bad attitude.

Your interviewers are judging how quickly you'll be productive if hired, and how well you'll fit with the team. Tell them multiple stories that show you can use the skills they identify as essential. Expect to tell relevant stories in different ways until you sense they hear you. Just 7 percent of their attention is on your words, so choose them wisely!

> **66** *If you just focus on getting your job done and being a good colleague and a team player in an organization, and are not focused on being overly ambitious and wanting pay raises and promotions and the like . . . the rest of it all takes care of itself.* **99**
>
> —Richard Anderson, former CEO of Delta Air Lines

Interview the Interviewer

Even in a hiring interview, you are still assessing the job. You need to know the following: Does this job fit me? Does it use many of my strengths? Am I comfortable with the people I've met?

Ask yourself the following questions:

1. *Do I want to work with these people?* Pay attention to your intuition. Sometimes your interviewer will give all the "right" answers to your questions, but you'll still have an uneasy feeling. Don't ignore that feeling. You want an environment where you'll thrive. Author and venture capitalist Guy Kawasaki put it starkly: "When you work for someone else, your real job is to make your boss look good." Before committing to a job, ask yourself "Is this person someone I want to make look good?" If the answer is no, keep looking.

2. *Can I do this job? Do I want to do this job?* In chapter 1, we introduced "can-do" skills and "want-to" skills. What skills are most needed in this job? Are they skills you love to use repeatedly, or just once in a while?

3. *Can I persuade the organization that I'm different from other applicants?* Formulate an answer to this question before you walk into the interview. Weave in what you know about the company's needs as you talk about your work style and experience.

Keep in mind that interviewers are as scared as you are during the hiring interview. They don't want to make a hiring mistake. Companies have tales of many hiring misadventures. Your interviewer does not want to become a company legend for making a big hiring mistake!

REALITY CHECK

It used to be that hiring for higher paying jobs on the career track never happened without second interviews. If unemployment rates are low, applicant pools are small, or there's a rush to fill jobs, job offers can happen after just one interview. While the following questions may seem a bold or cocky, they need to be asked before you accept a job offer:

1. Can you recall someone in this job who was a bad fit? What characteristics made them a poor fit for the job?

   You can also ask this question from the positive side, "Do you recall an employee that was a really good fit in this job? What made them so?"

   What you are looking for is information that will tell you if you are going to be a good fit.

2. How many hours a week do you expect someone in this position to work?

   If a position has been advertised as 40–45 hours a week, but management really wants you to work twice that, you need to know!

3. How often does this company give salary raises to employees? Is there a formal process and timing, or do they happen at-will?

   Good companies want to keep good workers. One way to do that is to give competitive starting salaries and have transparent policies for promotions, raises, and bonuses.

4. What kind of professional benefits do you offer?

   Employees who grow their skills become more valuable. Things such as whether a company provides opportunities for your professional growth or offers financial reimbursement for classes can influence what job offer you accept. If you are driven to excel, you want to be in an environment that will support your drive.

Interview-Ending Finesse

If the interviewer's questions move from the past toward the future, the interview is going well. Make time to ask the following four questions before the end of the interview. Don't be afraid to speak up—you need the answers to these questions.

1. Can you offer me this job? (If you want the job, be sure to ask for it; 20 percent of people who ask for a job get it.)

2. Do you want me to come back for another interview, perhaps with some of the other decision-makers here?

3. When may I expect to hear from you?

4. What is the latest I can expect to hear from you?

If it becomes clear that the interviewer doesn't view you as qualified for this particular job, don't assume all is lost. Be sure to ask these three questions before you bolt for the door:

5. Do you have questions about my qualifications to do this job? (This gives you a chance to make another pitch about your strengths. Make sure your response addresses your interviewer's specific concern.)

6. Are there other jobs in your department for which you think I'm qualified?

7. Are there other departments that might hire me?

After an Interview

Always send a thank-you note to your interviewer. If more than one person was involved in the interview, send a note to each person on the interview team. (See chapter 4 to review thank-you note basics.)

- Thank each interviewer for their time.

- If you enjoyed meeting the interviewer, say so.

- Mention one or two of your skills, training, or previous jobs that best show your ability to do the job.

Be succinct. A letter of just three or four paragraphs (with two to four sentences in each paragraph) can be read quickly and won't sound like a sales pitch instead of a thank-you. Always make certain your note—whether sent by USPS or emailed—is grammatically correct, with no spelling errors. Send it within twenty-four hours of your interview.

Here's a thank-you note sample:

> *(Date)*
>
> *Dear Mr. Monroe:*
>
> *Thank you so much for interviewing me for the job of nurse's aide. I was so impressed that you took the time to show me around and introduce me to other employees.*
>
> *My training makes me very qualified for this job. I hope you agree. My experience helping my grandmother after her last surgery taught me how to work with older patients who are sick or slightly confused.*
>
> *I hope I'll hear from you on Friday, as you indicated. If not, I'll call you next week.*
>
> *Sincerely,*
>
> *Sean Jones*

PARACHUTE TIP:

Don't overthink writing a thank-you note. Learn a good structure you can use over and over. Find more templates with an internet search for "job interview thank-you notes."

Don't Get Discouraged

If your faith in finding a really great job is flagging, ask your contacts to connect you with other young people who have found good first-career jobs. Ask a few of these successful young job-earners how they did it. Can you adapt what they did to your job search? Find and read inspiring books or articles on people who love their work. If your faith in finding any job in your field is floundering, ask your contacts if they know of someone who has been hired in the last six months (they usually do) and talk with these newbies. Other people's stories can help you stay positive.

Remember, not many get an ideal job in their first attempt. While we encourage you to go after the exciting job of your dreams, it can take several jobs in your favorite field before you can even define, much less get, that perfect job for you. But if you don't look for one, you'll never find one. It takes lots of steps and hard work. Each time you have a setback, give yourself time to reexamine your strategy and goal, and revamp as needed. Then redouble your efforts to find people doing the work you hope to do—the younger in age, the better. If these people encourage you, you probably have the right stuff. If you have the right stuff and work hard to get hired, you will succeed.

Practice answering common hiring interview questions out loud. You need to get comfortable hearing yourself talk about you. Speak clearly. Craft your responses to be no more than two minutes long. Longer responses can come across as monologues. You'll be amazed at how much information you can communicate in 120 seconds. Breathe and center yourself before answering important questions. Take a few seconds to think out two or three important points to cover with your answer.

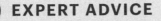

Interview Tips for Those with Disabilities: Your Chance to Shine

By Elisabeth Sanders-Park, President of WorkNet Solutions
https://www.linkedin.com/in/elisabethsanderspark/
elisabeth@worknetsolutions.com

If you have an interview, the employer believes you can do the job, even if you need some training. Employers do not spend time interviewing people without the basic qualifications. During the interview, they will verify your skills and explore if you are a good fit—that means having the right presentation, attitude, dependability, motivation, and network. Here are some tips on how to shine in the interview so they want to hire you:

LEARN THE COMPANY: Companies like to be chosen. They won't hire you just because you need work or have the skills they are looking for. Do your homework. Get to know the company's mission, products/services, target customers, and culture. Prepare to tell them why you want to work for them. Be specific. Have you heard good things? Are you a happy customer? Let them know you want to use your skills to bring their mission to life!

KNOW YOURSELF: This is your chance to tell them what you have to offer. Prepare to respond to "Tell Me About Yourself" by stating your name, two to three things that make you great, and thanking them for in the interview. For example: "My name is Lisa. I have two years' experience in retail customer service including training new associates. I love to help people find what they are looking for, and at least twice a week someone comments on my friendliness. I'm looking forward to building your brand and my career. Thanks for inviting me to interview."

LOOK GOOD: You have just eight seconds to make a great first impression. Dress like a top performer in the job you want (being overdressed is better than being underdressed). Be sure your hair, nails, skin, and teeth look good. For a virtual interview, position the camera just above eye level, light yourself from the front, and arrange a simple, professional background. Throughout the interview, keep your face relaxed and pleasant and look directly at the interviewer.

ROCK YOUR FIT: Focus on and highlight the skills, education, and experience you bring to the job.

EDIT YOURSELF: Answer the questions. Share stories and examples of how you will do the job well, make them more money than you cost, fortify their team, and delight their customers—but avoid giving too much information (or TMI). Employers are not allowed to ask about most personal issues—if you have a car, are married, or have children, your sexuality, religion, politics, mental health issues, and more—but many people share without thinking. Keep your focus on the job.

DOES THE EMPLOYER NEED TO KNOW? You may be asked if you have a disability that will keep you from performing the job responsibilities. The answer should always be no, because you should not apply for job you cannot do. Of course, you may need a "reasonable accommodation" (in accordance with the American Disability Act, www.usdoj.gov/crt/ada) to do the job well. Many people ask for accommodations, even if they do not have a diagnosed disability. You can discuss this with HR once you are hired. You can choose to disclose a disability sooner if you want—this makes sense if the disability is apparent during the interview. The employer may also discover it while reviewing your work history (i.e., you have left a job in the past because of it). Otherwise, the general rule of thumb is to wait to discuss it with HR once you are hired.

LISTEN ACTIVELY: Show your interest in the job and company, and your respect for the interviewer, by making eye contact, smiling slightly, leaning in a bit and nodding. If it is helpful and comfortable for you, take a few notes so you can ask questions. If it's a virtual interview, be sure to mention that you are taking notes (and not just looking down), or position your notepad so they can see it.

GET THEM TALKING: An interview should be 50/50: both parties should be talking and answering questions as you are each are interviewing the other to see if this is a fit. Prepare to ask questions and request examples during the interview by saying, "Can you say a little more about that?" Be curious. If you are wondering about something, ask the question. You may also ask what the interviewer likes about the company, what makes a person ideal for the job, specifically how you can make the company money and promote their mission if you get the job, and what more they need to know about you to hire you.

RELAX AND ENJOY: Once you get to the interview, there is nothing more you can do to prepare but take a deep breath and be present. Stay calm. Trust yourself. And show them why they will be glad to have you on the team.

You're Hired! Now What?

Congratulations! That hard work paid off and you've been hired. Did you get a written copy of your job offer? If this job is starting you on your career path, get a written job offer. Compare what you were told verbally with the written offer. Bring up any discrepancies to your hiring manager before you sign a contract.

Over the next few weeks, let your contacts and professional network know your job hunt has been successful. Enjoy your good news and be sure to celebrate all your efforts.

As you start your new job, is there something else you should be doing? The late author and creative job-search pioneer John Crystal once said, "To take charge of your career, you need to look further down the road than headlight range. You need to begin your next job hunt the day you start your current job."

Oof! That's probably not what you wanted to hear right now. But taking charge of your next career move is simply a continuation of what you've already been doing. What's your next step on the way to your ideal job? What training or education will you need? What kind of a work portfolio do you need to build from your current job?

To help you find the next job on your career path, we have a few more recommendations for you.

Keep a Job Journal

Each week, spend ten-to-fifteen minutes making notes about what you did during the week. Is Friday after lunch perfect for updating? Jot down names of projects, tasks, activities, or important meetings. Make notes about what to include in a future job portfolio. Mark what you like with a +, and use a - for job duties you didn't like. Include committees you've been asked to serve on and the names of professional organizations you've joined. Note any offices you may hold in professional organizations.

Why do this weekly? All new hires think they will never forget the details of their first big job. But in six months, your memory blurs. If you write down all the tasks and responsibilities of your regular job duties and special projects, you won't forget you did them. Your job journal will help with performance reviews and self-evaluations, and will put you ahead of the game when you make your next strategic career move.

Who's in the C-Suite?

The C-suite is a term for corporate executive positions. If you've been hired in a corporation, make sure you know who they are. Meet everyone in your department within your first week. We know you're just trying to keep your head above water, but you never know when you'll need someone else to help you finish a project or task. Being labeled "that standoffish new hire" is not going to help you.

As you become familiar with your new work environment, begin to meet and observe people throughout the organization. Who are the up-and-comers? Is there a manager you would rather work for, or a division you would rather work in? Get to know the people who have the jobs you want. Get to know their managers too. Don't say, "I want your job"; you won't build good relations with your colleagues that way. Do ask people about the specifics of their jobs. By doing information interviews at work, you can develop a plan for the next step in your career.

Watch, Listen, and Learn

If you join a business, division, or department that has two or more people, you're entering a situation that has a history. Find out that history. There are ongoing dynamics and power struggles you don't know about yet. As you learn your way around, observe everyone and everything. Don't overshare personal information, go out for drinks, or get overly friendly until you know someone's motives. It's a fact of modern life that between church attendance waning and pandemics happening, we have fewer options for meeting new people. It's tempting to let coworkers fill social needs. Go slow. After a few weeks of watching the scene, you'll probably put together what's going on and whom you can trust.

Find a Mentor

In fact, find several mentors. If this is a company in which you hope to have a long-term career, find a mentor within the company. If you like the industry, find one or more mentors outside the company. You can pick people who are still working or who have retired. Choose mentors who have achieved the level of success that you want. Meet with your mentors at least twice a year.

We hope that after reading this chapter, you feel more confident—and maybe even more excited—about your first hiring interviews. There's a learning curve. Becoming a successful interviewee is a role. The more you practice, the more comfortable you'll get being interviewed. It just takes one great interview to get a job, and getting hired is an important step toward having the life you want.

CHAPTER 11

Trends and Your Career

> **❝** *The truth is, if you want a decent job that will lead to a decent life today you have to work harder, regularly reinvent yourself, obtain at least some form of postsecondary education, make sure that you're engaged in lifelong learning, and play by the rules . . . we terribly mislead people by saying otherwise.* **❞**
>
> Tom Friedman, author and *New York Times* columnist

Your career is under *your* command, but not always under your control. Although a few employers are known for their employee retention efforts, you can't expect your employer to plan your career advancement for you. Most employers aren't much interested in new employees' career development (though your managers pay attention to their own). Part of managing your career will include being aware of trends that could affect or derail your career. Trend is a noun and a verb. As a noun, "trend" refers to the general direction in which something is developing or changing. Used as a verb, it is similar: to change or develop in a general direction. Smart young adults keep their futures from being ambushed by keeping track of rising trends. Emerging economic, scientific, social, cultural, and global issues have the power to bring change or chaos into your life.

First, we'll cover global trends that will affect the job market. Then we'll look at what you can do to prepare for or mitigate their effects on your work life.

Megatrends

Megatrends will affect everyone; whether these are minor inconveniences or potentially devastating often isn't known until a trend has been going for a while. Megatrends bring about job market volatility. Here are the trends now in play:

- **CLIMATE CHANGE:** This is the sleeping giant of megatrends. It will cause huge volatility in the job market, increased immigration, and food insecurity.

   Investment in renewable sources of energy has outpaced investment in coal and oil. Green jobs have gone from outliers to necessity, as industries seek to become sustainable. For example: the cost of lumber for new construction has given rise to the use of 3D printers for making homes and commercial buildings out of specialized concrete, plastic, resins, plant matter, and post-consumer recycled materials.

- **AI, ROBOTICS, AND OTHER EMERGING TECHNOLOGIES:** While these job market game changers will create many jobs, these roles will be highly technical. Even entry-level jobs will need specific training. By 2030, an estimated forty-five million workers will have been displaced by automation.

- **ROBOTIC PROCESS AUTOMATION (RPA):** Workers with bachelor's and advanced degrees, specialized training, and high-level analytical skills feel protection from automation—but they are not. By 2021, 80 percent of corporate executives had implemented some form of RPA; expect an increase to nearly 100 percent by 2025. Professional work (medicine, law, finance, and tech) combines lots of time doing routine processing of information, with the occasional need for sensitive judgement. Creators of RPA think any process can be automated: For $10,000, a bot can be built to eliminate two-to-four human jobs.

- **BIG DATA:** In the last decade, data has grown by a mind-boggling 4300 percent. This both organized and unorganized data from social media platforms. Data is mined for customer preferences to reveal markets and products for future development.

- **DEMOGRAPHICS:** Millennials are now the largest generation in the workforce. In the United States, that workforce is older, grayer, and shrinking. Average retirement age is now sixty-four, but 54 percent of those over sixty-five intend to keep working. People who are physically fit question the wisdom of retiring at all. When older workers stay in jobs, younger workers can't move up.

- **GLOBALIZATION:** If current trends continue, half of the world's largest companies will be located in Brazil, India, Eastern Europe, or other emerging markets. From 2000 to 2010, world-wide competition caused 40 percent of Fortune 500 companies to fall off the list. These were replaced with new global companies.

- **EPIDEMICS AND PANDEMICS:** In 2020, COVID-19 morphed from regional outbreak to global threat. The illness has brought millions of deaths and personal human misery through unemployment and isolation. It has also revealed the weakness of supply chains dependent on one country or region for both raw and finished materials. Both the medieval plague and early twentieth-century Spanish flu caused more deaths, but disease traveled more slowly in previous centuries. With air travel, the most remote areas of the Earth can be reached in forty-eight hours.

Due to megatrends a field may grow or die off quickly. A growing industry or field generates new jobs and a shrinking industry reduces jobs.

Each megatrend has contributed to the need to redefine work. Google's current definition of job, "a paid position of regular employment," seems old-fashioned and not quite adequate to define the mix of gig, contract, freelance, and other work sources necessary to create adequate individual income.

PARACHUTE TIP

If you need to do a research paper for a class, why not learn which megatrends will impact the field you hope to work in, and how it will be affected? You may uncover facts that people with whom you had information interviews didn't know. This increases your value to would-be contacts.

Tracking Emerging Trends

Tracking emerging trends is important for choosing, developing, and keeping your career. Research keeps you informed. Information helps you create options. Having options is the best preparation for economic or social change. Early in the career-choice process, knowing the current trends in your favorite fields may affect whether you pursue a specific career. If you go into a field knowing the challenges ahead, you can make plans for how to respond to them. If you do this kind of research repeatedly during your work life, huge changes can't sneak up on you.

Your current job may fit you now, but all jobs are temporary. Keep your Parachute up-to-date and your professional network maintained. You will need both to change jobs quickly.

To stay employable in fast-changing job markets, your best defense is a good offense. To keep on a career track of *your* choice when the job market is volatile means you must:

- Keep your current job skills sharp.

- Add to them often to qualify for new careers in emerging fields.

- Find and investigate trends in your field. Know how they can impact your job. Make plans.

In truth, working people spend more time filing their nails than managing their careers or researching a strategy to get and keep jobs they like. Recruiters and executive coaches suggest that their clients write a new resume each New Year's Day, whether they are job hunting or not. Although updating your resume at least annually is a good idea, it's not much of a strategy for keeping or advancing in your career.

Keeping track of new jobs that interest you and trends emerging in your own field is a much better use of your time. Talking with your mentors and colleagues, and attending professional conferences are efficient ways to track industry changes. Some workplace skills are in constant demand. For other skill sets, demand appears to ratchet up or disappear overnight. You may find a future career move will be into a job that only recently morphed into reality.

PARACHUTE TIP

If you want to keep up with what you need to know to stay employed, you'll need to read about workplace trends. Read a top financial or economics periodical, or blog at least once a quarter. IT workers, social media marketers, and others need to read about their field daily or weekly. If your field moves slower, set aside time at least once a month to catch up.

Sustainable Careers

The words "sustainable" and "sustainability" may be well known to you, and you will certainly hear them more in the coming years. Something is sustainable if it can easily be maintained and renewed over time. The term also refers to the use of natural resources without depleting them or destroying the environment.

What is a sustainable organization or business? To be considered sustainable or green, here are some basic criteria:

- Complies with all environmental regulations
- Conserves energy and water
- Prevents pollution
- Reduces, reuses, and recycles
- Uses renewable energy
- Responsibly measures, controls, and reduces the organization's carbon footprint

In recent years, the concept of sustainability has permeated our personal and work lives. Sustainability has many implications for your work life. Careers have to be sustainable; otherwise, they can weaken and die. The cost of education after high school, living expenses, any debt for education, and your starting salary must all be factored into deciding whether a particular career or job choice is sustainable for you.

National Geographic lists these as the fastest-growing green jobs:

- Urban growers (think rooftop gardens and converted storage containers)
- Water quality technicians
- Clean car engineers
- Recyclers
- Natural scientists
- Green builders
- Solar cell technicians
- Green design professionals
- Wave energy producers
- Wind energy producers
- Biofuel jobs

REALITY CHECK

Are you living a sustainable life? To learn the size of your ecological footprint, take the quiz at https://www.footprintcalculator.org

Discover Career Trends

What are the top trends in your favorite fields? To discover what challenges you must track, let's pull some information together.

- List any issues you recall being mentioned in your information interviews about where the field is going, what kinds of jobs are emerging, and what's being phased out.

- If your town is big enough to have a chamber of commerce, ask someone there about trends in your field. If your area has a workforce program (or what used to be known as county or state employment office), someone there may know of trends in the fields or industries where you want to work.

- Do an online search to find changes or challenges to jobs, fields, or industries you are considering.

- Read two or three of the professional journals for your field or industry. Check out articles in *The Economist* and the London *Financial Times*.

  What trends are cited?

  When are they expected to come into play?

  What are some projections about how this will affect a field or industry?

- Ask your contacts in the field for accurate information about where things are headed.

  Do this research for your top three fields or jobs. Are there trends shaping up that might shift your educational goals or make you not want to pursue a job in any one of these fields?

Personal Financial Sustainability

The jobs or job cluster you are considering must be financially sustainable. A job that is financially sustainable covers your bills, those of your dependents, and allows for saving and having fun. The definition of sustainable given earlier as "something that is easily maintained" applies to you too. If your combined student loan and credit card debt exceeds two-thirds of your starting salary, you won't find it easy to maintain your life.

Not all training programs, majors, or college degrees are sustainable when earnings, education costs, debt, and time out of the workforce are considered. There are dozens of jobs that need a bachelor's degree that pay little more than minimum wage. The top 25 percent of high school graduates make more money than the bottom 25 percent of university graduates. There are graduate school programs that increase student debt but do little to increase earnings.

As you make decisions about the kind of work you want to do, consider how much the training, internships, or education you need to qualify will cost you. Realistically, how long will those studies take if you have to work "part-time"? "Full-time"? If the necessary studies will put you in debt for more than 33 percent of the annual starting salary, that choice is not financially sustainable. This doesn't mean you should permanently give up a career path because it is too expensive to pursue at the moment. You may need to come up with an alternative strategy—such as deciding to take a job that's not a career goal, but you like it well enough to stay several years while saving money to pursue your ideal career.

Job Market Volatility

Job market volatility should be expected. Globally, the next decade is not likely to be a calm one. There's just too much political and economic turmoil happening now. How those upheavals will affect financial and job markets in the United States and other countries is not known. It's best to keep your skills sharp, attend the best training you can afford, and get a side hustle going. A side hustle is work you take on in addition to your full-time job, something you offer as a product or service. A side hustle gives you another income stream. Avoid side hustles that are multilevel marketing or make you purchase expensive inventory. A side hustle can keep you afloat if your main job disappears. You can learn about side hustles through books, YouTube videos, podcasts, and TED Talks. Spend some of your online time learning about side hustles and how they can increase your financial sustainability.

Your Parachute doesn't equate to just one job. The factors you've listed describe attributes of *many* jobs. To stay sustainable, whether you're just starting out or in the middle or your work life, you will want to know at least three different jobs for which you are well matched. If your current career path abruptly ends, you've got a backup plan ready to roll out.

CHAPTER 12

Beyond Your Dream Job: Create the Life You Want

> 66 *Be yourself. Everyone else is already taken.* 99
>
> —Oscar Wilde, Irish poet and playwright

You've heard the saying "There's more to life than work." While the focus of this book is to prepare you to find a terrific job, there's a deeper purpose: to help you get the whole life you want.

In this chapter, we invite you to explore what that whole life means for you. There are exercises for you to reflect upon the people, things, and activities that you want to include in your life. Next, you'll delve a bit deeper to consider the underpinnings of your life, your values and beliefs, and your "philosophy of life." After that, you'll examine people you respect and admire—your role models—and consider how they can help you become the person you want to be. Lastly, look at your purpose or mission in life. What are you on earth to do? The Discovery Exercises in this chapter ask you to spend time reflecting on different aspects of your life—how you want to live, and what type of person you want to be. Although you can learn from how your friends and other people answer these questions, to get the life you want, you must know the answers for yourself.

> **If you don't take the time to work on creating the life you want, you're eventually going to be forced to spend a lot of time dealing with a life you don't want.**
>
> —Kevin Ngo, author and motivational speaker

Envision Your Life, Design Your Future

By reading this book and doing the Discovery Exercises, you can now describe your ideal job. Maybe you even know names of several jobs that match your Parachute. But what else do you want? How do you want to fill hours outside of work? What is most important to you about being alive? What kind of life do you want? Knowing what you want is the first step toward making that life happen. Don't expect these ideas to just pop into your head; it will take focused thought. Do you want your life to include . . .

- Friends, family, a life partner, children, pets?

- Sports and outdoor activities?

- Cultural activities (theater, music, dance)?

- Travel and time for hobbies?

- Involvement with community or religious organizations?

- Participation in political or environmental causes?

There are many more things you can do with your time outside work. This short list is to get you thinking what you want in your life—what you enjoy doing now and want to continue doing. Is anything missing from your life that you want in your future? What matters is that you become aware of how you want to spend your time. That way, you'll be sure to carve out enough time to enjoy the activities that make you happy.

What kind of family life do you want to have as an adult, particularly in relation to your work? Will it be like the family life you have now, or will it be different? Kyle, age fifteen, wants something different because, as he puts it, "My dad hides out at work." Family life often gets neglected these days. Prepandemic quality family time together averaged just forty minutes a day! If you want to have children, what kind of parent do you want to be? What kind of relationships do you want to have with your children?

The following exercise will help you envision your future and the way you want to live your life, including what and whom you want to play a part in it.

Picture Your Ideal Life

Having a picture of what you want your life to be is important for making it reality. Pretend a magic wand has been waved over your life, giving you everything that's important to you. Have fun with this, but give yourself plenty of time to think about what matters most. It may take days or a few weeks complete this exercise. Let what's really important to you rise to the surface. The goal is to have a visual image of your ideal life ten years from now. Once you are satisfied with the picture you create, hang it up where you can see it. As other ideas for the life you want arise, add them to your Ideal Life Picture. You'll need the following materials for this exercise (and your computer graphic art skills too):

- A large piece of white paper
- Colored pencils or pens
- Old magazines that you can cut up
- Scissors
- Glue

You may start with a simple list. Eventually, use pictures, symbols, or create a collage to express visually the kind of life you want.

The following questions will get you thinking about what you want to include in your picture. Don't limit yourself to ideas from the list; add whatever is important to you.

- In your ideal life, where do you live (city, suburb, rural area, on an island, in the mountains)?
- What kind of house or living space do you want? Solar energy? Off the grid? Loft space?
- Who is with you (friends, family, pets)?
- Where do you work? What do you do for a living?
- Do you travel? Where do you want to go? Where do you vacation?
- What activities—sports, cultural, religious/spiritual, family, community—do you participate in?

Work on your picture until you feel it truly represents the life you want. Now, look at your picture again.

Identify which bits are absolutely essential, which are wonderful but can wait, and which bits you could barter away to get what's really important.

What do you need to do to help make this ideal life happen? Because you can't do everything at once, choose one area that you can make happen now, or soon. Return to chapter 7 to review how to set short-term and long-term goals. Keep challenging yourself to bring to life those parts of your picture that make you very happy.

Once you have a concrete vision of your future, let's explore more deeply how you want to live that life and who you want to be. This includes discovering your unique contributions to the world, and finding meaning in your life and in the world around you. As you live, love, and learn more about life, you'll form a (spoken or unspoken) life philosophy, a way in which you understand and view life events and people.

A philosophy of life helps you to interpret and understand your life experiences, and to make decisions. Know what is important to you? Your beliefs will be reflected in your decisions. For some, the meaning of life may be grounded in religious or spiritual beliefs, and the interaction of those beliefs with life experiences; for others, it grows directly from their life experiences. We invite you to take twenty minutes now to think about your philosophy of life. Completing the exercise will take a bit longer. This exercise isn't a one-off; try to come back to it every couple of years. You'll notice that some of your values are constant, and some change.

Your philosophy of life shapes everything that you do, everything you are, and what you become. It shapes all aspects of your life, whether you are aware of it or not. If you aren't happy with your life, perhaps your philosophy needs a tune-up. Just as you created a concrete vision of your future by creating a picture of your ideal life, writing out your philosophy of life will help you recognize the values by which you want to live. Knowing what you want is the first step to making it happen.

> 66 *The goal of life is to make your heartbeat match the beat of the universe, to match your nature with Nature.* 99
>
> —Joseph Campbell, mythologist and author

PARACHUTE TIP

Let John Legend inspire your thinking. Watch the Grammy winner give a college commencement speech entitled "Finding Your Truth: Living a Soulful Life" at www.youtube.com/watch?v=NSIQszUAvow. This video was filmed over ten years ago. It has aged well.

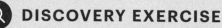

Writing Your Philosophy of Life

Everyone needs an "operating manual" for their life. That's what a philosophy of life is: it identifies what you value most in life, and articulates how those values guide your decisions.

Begin by writing down what is most important to you (family, friends, money, art, freedom, chocolate-chip cookies, or whatever). Why are these important to you? Why do you want them to be a part of your life? This exercise overlaps with the previous exercise—friends and family may come up in both exercises, for example. That's fine. Now, go a bit further and think about particular qualities that are important to you, such as truth, integrity, peace, compassion, or forgiveness.

Next, list the beliefs by which you intend to live your life (for example, all people are created equal, creation is sacred, or love is more powerful than hate). How will you face difficult times in your life? How do you hope you'll react to obstacles that may block your goals? How will you deal with loss, frustration, physical disability, or death?

Take time to think about what you value and believe. Think about what makes your life meaningful. Work on your philosophy of life for ten minutes a day for a week, or spend some time on it each weekend for a month or two. What emerges as you reflect on these important matters? Your philosophy of life will evolve and grow as you do. Revisit and revise your philosophy of life from time to time.

If you're ever disappointed with yourself or your life, ask yourself these questions:

- Am I paying attention to what I value most?

- Am I living my life guided by what I believe most deeply?

If you hit a rough patch in life, reviewing your philosophy of life will help you assess what went wrong and give you ideas to get back on track.

Do what you feel in your heart to be right—for you'll be criticized anyway. . . . In the long run, we shape our lives, and we shape ourselves. The process never ends until we die. And the choices we make are ultimately our own responsibility.

—Eleanor Roosevelt, diplomat and activist

Become the Person You Want to Be

As you picture your ideal life and articulate your philosophy of life, you may also want to reflect on what kind of person you want to be. Lisa, age fifteen, wants to be an adult who doesn't spend all her life at work: "Sometimes adults make it seem like all they do is work. That doesn't make being an adult very attractive." What makes being an adult attractive to you?

When you think about the person you want to be, you'll undoubtedly think about people who are important to you—people who have helped, inspired, befriended, or supported you through tough times. Who are the people you respect and admire? Who are your role models? Are they people you know, or celebrities? Identify people who, through their lives and example, can help you become the person you want to be.

Those who preserve their integrity remain unshaken by the storms of daily life. They do not stir like leaves on a tree or follow the herd where it runs. In their mind remains the ideal attitude and conduct of living. This is not something given to them by others. It is their roots. . . . It is a strength that exists deep within them.

—Anonymous Native American

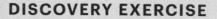
My Role Models

Take a sheet of paper and turn it so that the long edge is horizontal. Fold the sheet in half, crease it, and then fold it in half again. You should have four columns of equal width.

Title the first column "Names of people I admire." Under that heading, make a list of people you admire. These can be real people you know or have known, historical figures, or fictional characters from books, movies, comic books, or TV.

Title the second column "What I admire about them." Think about each person in the first column, then write down what you admire about them.

Title the third column "Do I have this trait?" Read over the traits you've written for each person you admire. Ask yourself, "Do I have this trait? Do I want to have this trait?" Write your answers in the third column.

Label the last column "How can I develop this trait?" Answer this question for each trait or attribute you'd like to develop or strengthen.

Reflecting on the traits you value—those that you most admire in other people—can help you cultivate those traits in yourself. Arrange to talk with one or more of your role models about a trait of theirs that you particularly admire: their compassion, intellect, wit, honesty, or ability to make people feel comfortable. Ask them how they developed that trait. Who are their role models? Do they have suggestions to help you develop that trait in your own life?

Purpose versus Passion

You may have heard adults talking about using passion to find an ultimate career or job fit. Awkward, yes, but they mean well. Research has found that purpose, not passion, is the #1 indicator of life satisfaction. Passions change. You know that. The singer, band, or video game that was the focus of your life three or four years ago—or the posters that took pride of place on your bedroom walls—have likely changed. Purpose is a steadier foundation upon which to build career and life choices.

Check out what former NFL player Trent Sheldon has to say about the power of purpose on episode two of his podcast *Straight Up* titled "How to Find Your Purpose" (https://podcasts.apple.com/us/podcast/straight-up-with-trent-shelton/id1489061681?i=1000459278706).

The Power of Vision

Successful people believe in the power of vision. They craft visions of what they want to create or make happen, and they apply these ideas to their personal and professional lives.

So here's your chance to be a movie or video director. If you were to create a movie of your life, from now through achieving your dreams or even your death, what would it be like?

Would your story be a romantic comedy? Anime or animation? Computer graphics or stop-motion? Drama? Sitcom? Stand-up routine? Musical? Docudrama or MTV? How would you organize episodes about your accomplishments, different decades, ah-ha moments, and hard-won wisdom? How would you show your future? (No tragedies—to prevent your life from becoming a tragedy, you think things out before doing them.)

Write a script for your story. Start with yourself from the present onward.

- What happens in your life as you age? What higher education do you choose?

- Who do you work for (yourself or an employer)? Who do you work with? Where do you work? Where do you live?

- What do you do at work? What do you do with your free time?

- What brings the most joy to your life?

- What obstacles do you encounter? How do you overcome them?

- Block out the scenes. Add director's notes for who does what in each scene.

- Work and rework your script until you feel it's ready to be enacted.

- Who will you get to play the different characters?

Roll cameras!

Discover Your Life Purpose or Calling

You may hear someone say, "I don't consider what I do *work*; it's my calling." Some want to feel that they are honoring their own talents and doing work that is more than earning money, even if they are earning money doing a job that is perfect for them. Having a calling is frequently rooted in religious or spiritual traditions. But those without religious beliefs can also feel the need to use their gifts in deeply meaningful ways. For those who believe this way, finding their calling becomes a high priority.

Is having a sense of purpose through your work, or finding a calling, important to you? Reading this book, doing the Discovery Exercises, and reflecting on how you want to live your life, what you deeply value, and whom you most admire can help you uncover your unique purpose for being here on Earth. The reflections you've done through this book can help you discover your life purpose or calling.

Perhaps you will be helped by this definition. American theologian Frederick Buechner defines vocation as the "place where your deep gladness and the world's deep hunger meet." Find your calling by doing what makes you deeply happy, while also meeting the needs of the world. Whether you seek a calling or work you enjoy, always remember that you have gifts to offer the world. The gift you are and the gifts you offer are unique. Only you can be you. What unique gifts of yours can make the world a better place?

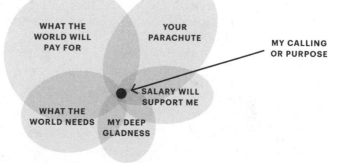

> **My mission in life is not merely to survive, but to thrive; and to do so with some passion, some compassion, some humor, and some style.**
>
> —Maya Angelou, poet

Dream life and work are not unicorns. They can be found. Timothy Forderer and I became mutual fans after learning that he had dropped off copies of this book to schools on Komodo Island. Captain Forderer is an example of someone who knows his philosophy of life, lives it, and has found his calling. Let his story inspire you to find and live yours.

Do What You Love and Do Some Good Along the Way

By Captain Timothy Forderer
Program Development Partner, The Wonderment
Timforderer@outlook.com

With the sudden death of my father came a serious wake-up call to live each day fully. I left my secure telecommunications career in 2001 to pursue a lifelong passion for sailing. In the process, I discovered another passion—being of service.

As a yacht captain, I saw my job as more than managing the yacht. I saw my purpose as curating experiences that would create memories that would last a lifetime for the owners and guests. Looking at my job in this way, I realized that my purpose was about being of service, and I saw this as an awesome responsibility and opportunity.

During my time creating memorable experiences on sailing-yacht *Vivid*, I traveled to some of the most remote places on the planet. Often, I found it was unsettling arriving at a destination in a several million-dollar yacht, and seeing the poverty of the people. I gained a better perspective on life, not only being grateful for my life, but becoming inspired to be of service to others. I became connected with the organization YachtAid Global, a nonprofit organization of like-minded boaters who include service to others in their cruising agendas.

Here is a snapshot of what being of service looked like for me as I sailed around the world:

- Providing forty-five cases of basic school and health-care supplies to twenty different locations around the world

- Delivering 150 water filters to provide clean drinking water for 15,000 people in five years.

- Giving Inspirational "Do What You Love" talks to over 10,000 young adults all over the world that focused on the importance of making your life's work something about which you care deeply.

In 2017, I was humbled with the YachtAid Global (YAG) Humanitarian of the Year Award.

My last sail aboard the superyacht *Vivid* was from Miami to Palma Mallorca, Spain. During that 4,500-mile voyage, away from all noise and distractions, I reflected on the amazing past eleven years. I thought about the people I had met, and how much help is needed in these remote island communities. My next step was clear—find a way to inspire others in the boating community into humanitarian service. How could I stitch selfless service into the fabric of the superyacht industry by encouraging a culture of not only "Doing What You Love," but doing some good along the way?

The answer to that question came when my time on s/y *Vivid* was over. I spent a year of service as the Executive Director of YachtAid Global. Day one on the job, Hurricanes Irma and Maria struck the Caribbean Islands, and I was about to have my initiation.

Besides delivering tangible goods to island nations, YAG also has disaster management expertise, and this was an opportunity for them to take the lead and foster collaboration between others in the yachting community.

In coordinating NGOs [nongovernmental organizations], government ministries, and the yachting community, we managed to deliver 325,000 pounds of targeted aid to the fifteen affected Caribbean islands including 83,000 meals, 48,000 hygiene kits, and over 6,300 tools. Forty-four superyachts, some crossing from Europe for the purpose of helping, arrived laden with relief items including everything from baby food to plywood. With over 750 crew members and thousands of volunteers, the huge latent power of the superyacht industry had been harnessed for the first time. Its ability to do good on a large scale was both encouraging and inspiring.

Today I am continuing this mission to stitch selfless service into the very fabric of the world cruising community. I've recently partnered with an amazing nonprofit initiative called The Wonderment to create something I've dreamed of for a long time: an accessible, fun way for world-cruising kids to connect with each other and with local kids in the coastal communities they visit, while together making a difference and sharing it with the world. This group is the Band of Explorers. You can see more at www.thewonderment.com/BandofExplorers

We are eager for the next generation to learn how to make the world a better place. Complex issues such as climate change, international conflict, and massive inequality will need to be addressed. Bringing kids together from all parts of the world to discover their commonality is an important step in the process of solving world problems.

There is a critical need for everyone to contribute to making the world a better place. Our progress as a civilization can no longer afford people working just to earn a paycheck. So absolutely do what you love, what is meaningful to you, and what challenges you, but please find your selfless-service-sweet-spot and do some good along the way.

My Wish for You

In closing, I wish you well as you discover yourself, design your future, and live a life you love financed by work you enjoy. May you find work that challenges, satisfies, and delights. May that work be part of a whole life that is fulfilling in every way. May you share your unique gifts to make the world a better place.

As you move from teen to adult, I hope you will do the following: Tell the truth. Stand up for those who can't speak for themselves. Take some (manageable) risks. Be a bit cautious. Be generous, but have boundaries (there is joy in giving, but not in neglecting yourself). Be thorough. Be persistent. Be kind. Prepare to deal with the good and the disappointing parts of life. Live fully, love deeply. Pay attention to your decisions because with every one you make, you are creating your life and your future. The adventure of your life is waiting. Go find it.

Appendix

❝ *Kids should have more breathing room and more say in their life path.* **❞**

—Matteo Sloane, on what he hopes others learn from
the USC college admissions scandal

Parent Checklist: Steps to Success

Choosing a first career path is a multiyear process. A forty-five minute interest inventory given to high school sophomores isn't enough! To encourage and support your child's career development, below are some steps parents can take.

Elementary and Middle School

- During elementary and middle school, notice what your child is interested in and help them explore those topics and activities. Discuss the idea of earning a living. Discuss the jobs that might use your young teen's interests. YouTube has an extensive collection of videos about people's work.

- Make time to talk about careers and make it fun. For twenty minutes once a month, go on a walk, have tea or cocoa together, and talk about your own career history or jobs about which your child is curious.

Middle and High School

- Talk with your teen about your transition from after-school and entry-level jobs to your career now. Don't be afraid to tell them about career bloopers and missed opportunities.

- Are there other adults in your student's life, friends or relatives, who have dynamic careers or who have overcome significant obstacles to find work they enjoy? Ask if they will share about their work lives with your teen or tween. Take note of the people your child really connected with, as they might be a good mentor, no matter the field in which they work.

- Help your child learn some aspect of technology. If this isn't your forte, schools and communities have programs for this. Find one. Jobs are increasingly partnerships between humans and machines. If you find your child chafing about learning math or tech subjects, encourage them by
    » explaining how you use math or tech in your everyday life
    » rewarding them for persevering when a subject is hard or confusing
    » asking for help from school personnel or finding tutors for your child

- If your child is floundering in math, get help. Many US schools don't teach math well. Traditionally, math classes often focus on formulas and procedures rather than teaching students to think creatively about solving complex problems that involve all sorts of mathematics. Find an online or local course that teaches mathematics creatively or through the inquiry method.

- Enroll your child in a self-defense class. The world can be a tough place and teens are the most vulnerable of all workers.

- Have discussions with your child about your work activities and the effort, rewards, and challenges you face. If your job is satisfying, explain how fulfilling work improves your life. Emphasize the effort you put in to be effective and valuable at work.

- If possible, bring your child to your work site so that they can see the setting.

- Encourage your child's participation in some team activities in school or after school. Teamwork is highly prized by employers in all fields. Experiences on teams helps them to learn important life skills, such as cooperation, showing up, and following through.

- Let your teen know when you expect them to fully support themselves. Fifty percent of the parents of Millennials support their children's lifestyle—cell phones, rent, car insurance—to the detriment of their own.

Once in High School

- What apprenticeship opportunities are available to your student through their high school? When do students apply for them?

- At freshman parent orientation, find out if your student's school participates in the Armed Services Vocational Aptitude Battery (ASVAB), YouScience, or other ability testing and at what grade those tests happen. Natural abilities are different than knowledge or interests. It is extremely important that your teen's career choices take advantage of their innate abilities. Work shouldn't be a constant struggle.

- By the age of fifteen, your student should be able to name three fields that interest them.

- Aid your teen in finding job shadowing and internship opportunities.

- Begin a serious assessment of how much money your family can contribute to your child's higher education.

- By the age of sixteen, your student should know one to three job clusters in each of the fields that interest them.

- Look at FAFSA forms and scholarship applications to learn about requirements and deadlines.

- Six degrees of separation has now melted to two! Help your student find people to talk with about jobs that interest them. Your friends, their friends, service club members, booster club members, chambers of commerce, and other civic groups can help make connections. Through LinkedIn, Facebook, and Twitter your student can find people with whom to video chat. Make sure your teen knows about protecting themselves online. Check out all potential contacts. Being with your teen as they do these activities is good, but after the first few, let them take the lead.

- During the summer your teen is a rising senior:
  - » Update finances and inform your teen how much you can contribute to their continuing education. Be realistic. Don't commit resources that will harm your budget or retirement. Help your teen identify high-demand, entry-level jobs in their favorite field that take the least amount of study. Introduce the idea of cycles of learning, work, and more learning.
  - » Along with your teen, look at the Parachute Diagram (pages viii–ix). Research shows that people who enjoy their work know this information about themselves. Chapters 1 through 3 of this book will help your student fill in their Parachute. Chapter 4 covers how to use it. Read along with your teen so you can discuss questions and issues.
  - » Assist your teen in finding employers to talk with about options for gaining qualifications for their first career path. Employers have strong opinions about the skills they want.
  - » Help your teen create their multipart plan (see page 79). The goal of high school is not university; it is to set up your child to successfully transition from school to work at whatever education level that happens to be.

- Don't let your teen make career or education choices based on *something they heard somebody say.* Due diligence is the top risk-management strategy for a reason.

- Avoid most private and Parent Plus loans. Both have proven to be debt quicksand. Assist your student to choose first-career goals that limit borrowing to two-thirds of likely starting salary.

Remember:

- As an adult, unemployment is stressful because of the need to quickly find another paying job. High school is likely the only stretch of time that your teen will have the ability to investigate every job or career that interests them. Encourage them to use it. The information they discover will guide years of job searching.

- Your child will be in the world of work for fifty to sixty years. There is no reason a big, expensive, university degree acquired with too much debt needs to be their first level of qualification.

- Your child won't have a career in field X if they can't get a job in field X. Make sure your teen or young adult is familiar with and uses the tried and true effective job-search techniques covered in chapters 9 and 10.

- That a job might not exist in five to ten years is likely not on your teen's radar. It needs to be. Make sure it's a question your child asks.

Helpful Online Resources

- The Danville Area Community College has put together a helpful guide called the Parent Guide for Career Planning (https://www.dacc.edu/assets/pdfs/career/ParentGuideforCareerPlanning.pdf).

- You can read the latest on new collar jobs and apprenticeships for high school students in this article from the Brookings Institute, "The Business of Expanding Apprenticeships" (https://www.brookings.edu/events/the-business-case-for-expanding-apprenticeships-federal-and-employer-perspectives/).

- This article by the World Economic Forum, "Jobs of Tomorrow: Opportunities in the New Economy," covers emerging opportunities for employment (https://www.weforum.org/reports/jobs-of-tomorrow-mapping-opportunity-in-the-new-economy).

- Taking out federal loans? The *Wall Street Journal* article "Which College Graduates Make the Most?" compares schools and majors to see who has the most debt (https://www.wsj.com/articles/which-college-graduates-make-the-most-11574267424).

- Tempted to cut corners to get your teen into university? Check out the *Wall Street Journal* article titled "'Why Didn't You Believe in Me?' The Family Reckoning After the College Admissions Scandal" (https://www.wsj.com/articles/why-didnt-you-believe-in-me-the-family-reckoning-after-the-college-admissions-scandal-11579276312).

Excellent Websites

- Mysparkpath.com offers ways to talk with your teen about career choice.

- EUREKA.org has career information and helpful assessments.

- YouScience.com offers ability testing for senior high and middle school students. (YouScience has generously offered readers a 50% discount. Use the code PARACHUTE.)

Acknowledgments

Given the force with which it hit our lives, I must acknowledge COVID-19. The fallout from the pandemic will affect Gen Z's career and education opportunities for years. May this book give readers tools to overcome some of those challenges.

It takes dozens of people to publish a book. People who print, edit, index, design, handle accounts, sell, ship, and transport this book. Departments at both Ten Speed Press and Random House are involved. I'm sorry I haven't met all of you. To all who help get this book to readers, their parents, or teachers—a huge thank-you!

Special scoops of thanks to the Ten Speed team. Editor Ashley Pierce kept the many moving parts of the book's revision moving along like a Swiss watch. Well done! Want Chyi guided the book through the final stages of editing when Ashley took a temporary leave. Working with her has been a joy. Kaisha-Dyan McMillan is one clever copyeditor. She dropped unnecessary words while clarifying my intent. In the editing world, that's magic. Lauren Rosenberg created the new design for the fourth edition. Chloe Rawlins oversaw design production and cover. Dan Myers, production manager, coordinated the physical process for the manuscript to become a book.

I am grateful to the contemporary colleagues who contributed information and ideas for this edition. Rich Feller schooled me on the need to include abilities in the Parachute diagram. Mark Babbitt, Sumyyah Bilal, Shawn Cowley (LtColRet), Timothy Forderer, Elizabeth Harney-Sanders Park, Dan Schawbel, Patti Wilson, and Robin Roman Wright all gave their time to write essays for this edition or were interviewed. This book is stronger for their voices and wisdom.

Socorro Galusha-Luna assisted research, gave content advice, and read for content clarity. Nina Grayson, Berkeley English grad (and friend since we were eleven) was reader and grammarian. My late mother did this for the first two editions of this book, so I am doubly blessed that someone else dear to me has this skill set!

This edition was researched and written in 2020 and 2021. Difficult years for everyone and especially for my physician daughter, Serena Z. Brewer, DO. I am lucky in my daughter and grateful beyond words for her support and generous listening ear while I worked on the revision.

With love and gratitude,

Carol Christen
Parachute4teens@gmail.com
www.parachute4teens.org

About the Author

Carol Christen is a career strategist who has worked extensively with teenagers and young adults. She strongly feels that, in a country with few social safety nets, helping youth discover and get qualifications for well-paying, challenging jobs with advancement opportunities is an issue of social justice. Experience has taught her that the ability to get the best job one can in any job market is a survival skill every young adult needs to know. Contact Carol at parachute4teens@gmail.com or through her website www.Parachute4Teens.org.

INDEX

A

Abilities
  discovering, 9–12
  interests vs., 9
Ability tests, 10
ADHD, 26
AmeriCorps, 86
Apprenticeships, 65, 78–79, 85, 86
ASV-AB (Armed Services Vocational
    Aptitude Battery), 10
Attitude, importance of, 158–59

B

Best job fit
  as entrepreneur, 61
  exploring potential, 47–49
  five steps to, 137–43
  good enough vs., 137
  transferable skills and, 14
  Venn diagram of, 136
Boss, ideal, 33
Business etiquette, 119, 120

C

Career assessments, 31–32
Career coaching, 60
Career maturity, 66
Career planning
  benefits of, 1
  skills used in, 13
Careers
  awareness of possibilities for, 67–68, 85,
    115–16
  jobs vs., 47
  sustainable, 171–72
  trends and, 168–74
Career sites, 32
CEOs, traits of, 100
Certification programs, 89–90
Class assignments, 68–69
Clients, ideal, 33
Climate change, 169
Clothing, 144

Cold calling, 53
College
  alternatives to, 82–83
  budgeting for, 84, 91
  "business plan" for, 106–7
  career goals and, 91–92
  choosing, 107
  community, 72, 81, 84, 97
  costs of, 91–92
  debt and, 92, 94–98
  determining necessity of, 82–83
  earning power and, 96–97
  experience of, 108
  getting the most out of, 92–94
  graduation rates from, 72, 85, 91
  meaning of, 71
  selecting major in, 106, 108
Community, ideal, 35, 38–39, 40–41
Community colleges, 72, 81, 84, 97
Contacts
  cultivating, 100, 122–23, 125–26, 130,
    140–41
  examples of, 140
  See also Network building

D

Debt, 92, 94–98
Disabilities, 164–65
Discouragement, 162–63
Dual enrollment, 83

E

Education
  as an investment, 92
  need for, 84
  options for, 68, 72, 79–80, 82–83, 87–92
  See also Certification programs; College;
    High school; Trade schools
Email
  addresses, 117, 121, 131, 144
  thank-you notes by, 58
Entrepreneurs, 61
Epidemics, 170

R

References, 146
Remedial classes, 84
Responsibility, level of, 39, 42–43
Resumes, 147–50
Robotic process automation (RPA), 169
Role models, 180–81

S

Salary
    high, 91
    ideal, 39, 41–42
    information on, 39, 41
    of recent college graduates, 95–96
    researching, 95
Self-assessment, importance of, x, 5
Self-care, 150–51
Self-Directed Search (SDS), 30
Self-management skills, 23–26
Skills
    best, 13
    can-do vs. want-to, 22
    definition of, 13, 14
    desired by employers, 70, 99
    enjoyable, 13
    identifying, 15–22
    interests and, 13
    interpersonal (with people), 14, 17, 21
    job-search, 72–74
    knowledge (work content), 23–24
    mental (with information), 14, 17, 20
physical (with things), 14, 17, 19
    self-management (personal traits), 23–26
    soft, 105
    transferable (functional), 14, 22–23
Skill TIP boxes, 14, 19–21
Snapchat, 118
Social entrepreneurs, 61
Social media
    as career-planning tool, 122–33, 131–32
    characteristics of, 115
    downside of, 129
    popular sites, 118
    possibilities of, 115–16

safety and, 129–30
State Civilian Conservation Corps, 86
Student loans, 94–98
Summer work, 70–71
Sustainability, 86, 171–72, 174

T

Talents. *See* Skills
Tech sector, tips from, 77
Telephone calls, 144, 146
Thank-you notes, 58–59, 139, 161–62
TikTok, 118
To-do lists, 111, 113
Trade schools, 88–89
Twitter, 118, 128, 129

U

University Pages, 127–28

V

Vacancies, 146
Vision, power of, 182
Voicemail, 144

W

Web
    creating a presence on, 116–18,
        121–22, 131
    privacy and, 131–32
    See also Social media
Work environment, ideal, 35, 36–38
Work ethic, 99, 100
Work permits, 67

Y

YouTube, 118, 122, 129

Published in the United States by Ten Speed Press, an imprint of
Random House, a division of Penguin Random House LLC, New York.
TenSpeedPress.com
RandomHouseBooks.com

Ten Speed Press and the Ten Speed Press colophon are registered
trademarks of Penguin Random House LLC.

Earlier editions of this work were published in 2006, 2010, and
2015 by Ten Speed Press, an imprint of Random House, a division of
Penguin Random House LLC.

Icons used from thenounproject.com:
parachute by nareerat jaikaew (used for Parachute Tip boxes)
whistle by ProSymbols (used for "Do You Need a Career Coach?" box)
meter by Vectorstall (used for "job meter story" box)
closed book by David Glöckler (used for "business etiquette" box)

Library of Congress Control Number: 2021952749

Trade Paperback ISBN: 978-1-9848-5862-7
eBook ISBN: 978-1-9848-5863-4

Printed in the United States of America

Acquiring editor: Lisa Westmoreland | Project editor: Ashley Pierce
Designer: Lauren Rosenberg | Art director: Chloe Rawlins
Typefaces: Commercial Type's Graphik; NTC's Granite
Production designers: Mari Gill and Howie Severson
Production manager: Dan Myers
Copyeditor: Kaisha-Dyan McMillan
Proofreader: Jean Blomquist
Indexer: Ken DellaPenta
Publicist: Lauren Kretzschmar | Marketer: Monica Stanton

Fourth Edition

3rd Printing